West
Highlands

The author and publisher have made every effort to ensure that the information in this publication is accurate, and accept no responsibility whatsoever for any loss, injury or inconvenience experienced by any person or persons whilst using this book.

published by
pocket mountains ltd
6 Church Wynd, Bo'ness EH51 0AN
www.pocketmountains.com

ISBN: 0-9544217-5-2

Copyright © Pocket Mountains Ltd 2004

A catalogue record for this book is available from the British Library

All route maps are based on 1945 Popular Edition Ordnance Survey material and revised from field surveys by Pocket Mountains Ltd, 2002-04. © Pocket Mountains Ltd 2004. Maps on section introduction pages are based on map images © Maps in Minutes™ 2003. © Crown Copyright, Ordnance Survey 2003.

Printed in Poland

Introduction

This guide features forty circular walks in the West Highlands. It includes all of the Munros (peaks above 914m/3000ft) and many Corbetts (peaks over 762m/2500ft), as well as other hills that combine to make good circuits.

Routes have been chosen according to a number of factors, including variety of terrain, great views, historical interest, minimal road walking and the feasibility of a circular route.

Environmental factors such as the ability of access points to support additional cars and opportunities for bypassing visitor-sensitive or eroded areas have also been taken into account. Circular routes help to take the pressure off badly eroded paths, and walking in areas where there have been fewer footsteps is more conducive to natural regeneration of the land.

Walkers can also minimise their own impact on the environment by keeping to purpose-built paths whenever possible and walking in single file to help prevent widening scars. Restricting your use of bikes to tracks, parking sensibly, avoiding fires and litter, and keeping dogs on a lead, particularly on grazing land and during lambing, all help to preserve the land and good relations with its inhabitants. Many of the responsibilities for walkers are now enshrined in law.

How to use this guide

The routes in this book are divided into five regions. These divisions largely represent points of access into the mountains, or use natural geographical boundaries. The opening section for each of the five regions introduces the area, its settlements, topography and key features, and contains brief route outlines. It is supplemented by a road map, locating the walks.

Each route begins with an introduction identifying the names and heights of significant tops, the relevant Ordnance Survey (OS) map, total distance and average time. Many routes also contain an option for cycling part of the way where there is a long low-level approach.

A sketch map shows the main topographical details of the area and the route. The map is intended only to give the reader an idea of the terrain, and should not be followed for navigation.

Every route has an estimated round-trip time: this is for rough guidance only and should help in planning, especially when daylight hours are limited. In winter or after heavy rain, extra time should also be added for difficulties underfoot.

Risks and how to avoid them

Many of the hills in this guide are remote and craggy, and the weather in Scotland can change suddenly, reducing visibility to several yards. Winter walking brings particular challenges, including limited daylight, white-outs, cornices and avalanches. Every year, walkers and climbers die from falls or hypothermia in the Scottish mountains. Equally, though, overstretched Mountain Rescue teams are often called out to walkers who are simply tired or hungry.

Preparation for a walk should begin well before you set out, and your choice of route should reflect your fitness, the conditions underfoot and the regional weather forecasts.

None of the walks in this guide should be attempted without the relevant OS Map or equivalent at 1:50,000 (or 1:25,000) and a compass.

Even in summer, warm, waterproof clothing is advisable and footwear that is comfortable and supportive with good grips a must. Don't underestimate how much food and water you need and remember to take any medication required, including reserves in case of illness or delay. Many walkers also carry a whistle, first aid kit and survival bag.

It is a good idea to leave a route description with a friend or relative in case a genuine emergency arises: you should not rely on a mobile phone to get you out of difficulty. If walking as part of a group, make sure your companions are aware of any medical conditions, such as diabetes, and how to deal with problems that may occur.

There is a route for most levels of fitness in this guide, but it is important to know your limitations. Even for an experienced walker, colds, aches and pains can turn an easy walk into an ordeal.

These routes assume some knowledge of navigation in the hills with use of map and compass, though these skills are not difficult to learn. Use of Global Positioning System (GPS) devices is becoming more common but, while GPS can help pinpoint your location on the map in zero visibility, it cannot tell you where to go next.

Techniques such as scrambling or climbing on rock are required on only a few mountains in this guide. In winter conditions, take an ice axe and crampons – and know how to use them. Such skills will improve confidence and the ease with which any route can be completed. They will also help you to avoid or escape potentially dangerous areas if you lose your way. The Mountaineering Council of Scotland provides training and information.

For most of these routes, proficiency in walking and navigation is sufficient.

Access

Until the Land Reform (Scotland) Act was introduced early in 2003, the 'right to roam' in Scotland was a result of continued negotiations between government bodies, interest groups and landowners.

In many respects, the Act simply reinforces the strong tradition of public access to the countryside of Scotland for recreational purposes. However, a key difference is that under the Act the right of access depends on whether it is exercised responsibly.

Landowners also have an obligation not to unreasonably prevent or deter those seeking access. The responsibilities of the public and land managers are set out in the Scottish Outdoor Access Code.

At certain times of the year there are special restrictions, both at low level and on the hills, and these should be respected. These often concern farming, shooting and forest activities: if you are in any doubt, ask. Signs are usually posted at popular access points with details: there should be no expectation of a right of access to all places at all times.

The right of access does not extend to use of motor vehicles on private or estate roads.

Seasonal restrictions

Red and Sika deer stalking:
Stags: 1 July to 20 October
Hinds: 21 October to 15 February
Deer may also be culled at other times for welfare reasons. The seasons for Fallow and Roe deer (less common) are also longer. Many estates belong to the Hillphones network which provides advance notice of shoots.

Grouse shooting:
12 August to 10 December

Forestry:
Felling: all year
Planting: November to May

Heather burning:
September to April

Lambing:
March to May (Dogs should be kept on a lead at all times near livestock.)

Glossary
Common Gaelic words found in the text and maps:

abhainn	river
ailean	field; grassy plain
àirigh	summer hill pasture; shieling
allt	burn; stream
àth	ford
bàn	white
beag	small
bealach	pass; gap; gorge
beinn	ben; mountain
bràighe	neck; upper part
cìoch	breast; hub; pointed rock
clach	boulder; stone
cnoc	hillock
coire	corrie; cauldron; mountain hollow
creachann	exposed rocky summit
creag	cliff
cruach	heap; stack
dubh	black; dark
garbh	thick; coarse; rough
lagan	hollow; dimple
learg	hillside exposed to sea or sun
lochan	small loch; pool
meall	mound; lump; bunch
mór	big; great; tall
sgòrr	peak; cliff; sharp point
sgùrr	large conical hill
stùc	pinnacle; precipice; steep rock

Between the open sea and Loch Linnhe lie the lands of Ardgour, Sunart, Morvern, Moidart and Ardnamurchan. This peninsula of rugged terrain is guarded by mountains that rise abruptly from the sea: a place for only the most intrepid of traveller. It is not surprising that Bonnie Prince Charlie chose to gather his followers here to begin his ill-fated campaign in August 1745, or return to these secretive glens in flight after Culloden.

There are eight routes in this section, including a compact route on Gharbh Bheinn close to Corran, a low-lying walk over mixed terrain that joins the River Moidart, and a shorter excursion over Ben Hiant in volcanic Ardnamurchan. Two routes on the peninsula are accessible from the Road to the Isles or the railway to Mallaig: a high mountain circuit starting from Lochailort, and a route over mixed terrain that descends to Loch Shiel at Glenfinnan. Three further routes are just to the north of the peninsula in Morar. Two long circuits begin in Glenfinnan: one tackles the rocky spine of Streap, the other traverses a high ring of peaks. The final route makes an unusual horseshoe of Gulvain.

The Land of the Prince

Cliffs of Ardgour

Gharbh Bheinn Ⓖ (885m)

Walk time **4h40** Height gain **900m**
Distance **10km** OS Map Explorer **391**

Compact mountaineering route through a fine glen to discover high cliffs. The steep gully ascent demands respect and is a more serious undertaking in winter.

Start at a bridge over the Abhainn Coire an Iubhair, 500m west of the junction of the A861 and B8043 between Strontian and Corran (GR928597). From a loop of old road on the east side of the bridge, a path leads north to follow the river upstream. Although boggy at times, this glen gives easy walking with inviting glimpses of the high crags of the mountain. Once you have passed the rapids and a large boulder in the middle of the water, the river divides. Cross the northern tributary and follow the Allt a'Gharbh Choire Mhóir southwest, gaining height through a narrow ravine to emerge in the cauldron of Garbh Choire Mór. The diamond-shaped buttress of Gharbh Bheinn on the left (southwest) and two towers of Fiaclan Gharbh-Bheinn straight above

(WNW) make up the complex east face from this perspective. Aiming for the towers, begin a direct ascent of steep slopes. Pass left of the lower tower, which forms the northern boundary of the corrie, and keep left of the higher tower by following a narrowing gully. This emerges on the crest of the ridge. Bear southwards along the ridge over a few easy rock steps to start: gentler ground leads to the summit of Gharbh Bheinn (GR904622) (3h20). This is perched above vertical cliffs and care is required. From the top, walk west along a rocky terrace for 150m. Then descend southwards, following an easy ridge to a small bealach with cairn, and climb southeast to a smaller top composed of several humps. Descend ESE from here to pick up the prominent ridge of Sròn a'Gharbh Choire Bhig. This is rough going with many rocky folds and dips. Lower down, follow the path which drops in fits and starts to deposit you on the lower boggy reaches within sight of the bridge at the start (4h40).

Corran Narrows

Ferries of one sort or another have plied the short stretch of water at Corran for centuries. This is the gateway to the five areas of Ardgour, Morvern, Sunart, Moidart and Ardnamurchan and was on the original Road to the Isles used by cattle drovers to and from the islands. Hospitality has been offered here to travellers for hundreds of years at the Ardgour Inn. The present inn, incorporating three ferrymen's cottages, only dates back to the late 1740s, however: the original buildings were burnt down by Hanoverian troops to punish the locals who followed Bonnie Prince Charlie.

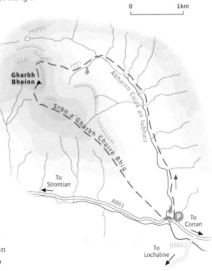

◀ Across Loch Linnhe to Gharbh Bheinn

9

Moidart gold

Creag nan Lochan (498m)

Walk time **5h40** Height gain **500m**
Distance **17km** OS Map **Landranger 40**

A low peak reached by intricate route-finding over many paths and tracks. This route follows a burn through a narrow ravine and across some complex topography, requiring good navigation.

Start at a picnic table, information panel and parking spot on a bend of the A861, 2km south of Ardmolich (GR723701). Walk west down the road for 200m to a minor road signposted for Dalelia. Take this road for 700m to a gate on the left. Pass through the gate and walk east to reach a junction after 500m. Take the left fork and follow

this track northwards, gaining gradual height. After 700m, a minor track joins from the right. Take this to cross a burn and pass through a gate: about 200m beyond, by a flat boulder, there is another fork. Turn left to accompany the Allt Ur northwards. The track fades near two long walls enclosing a plantation. Cross both walls, and then turn east to follow the main tributary of the Allt Ur. Higher up, the water, now flowing from the north, leads you through a tight gully laced with fool's gold. Climb up through this ravine, crossing from side to side of the burn as required, to reach a complex topography of bog and crags that make for hard walking. Follow the high ground northeast, passing small lochans, to climb

to the rocky knolls at the top of Coire na Taothuirt. Descend northwards to reach the crescent of Lochan na Creige. Follow the shoreline and then make the final ascent to the summit of Creag nan Lochan (GR758725) (3h). Take the north ridge to descend: this is fairly steep but requires no scrambling. The half-height crags are best avoided by keeping east. Descend northeast into Glen Forslan and to the head of a lochan. Follow the southern shore to find a track at the foot of the lochan which leads southwest to join a second track in Glen Moidart. This takes you downriver for 2km to a road that can be followed for 600m to two gates on the left. The further gate gives access to a good path. Follow this easily uphill, past General Ross's Cairn and over the apex of the ridge to reach the approach tracks. Return to the start (5h40).

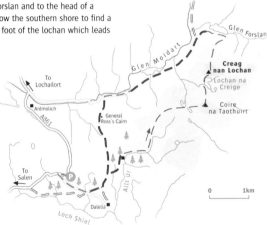

Somerled

The name of Acharacle is derived from the Gaelic 'Ath Thorguil' (Torquil's Ford); so called because Torquil, a Norse raider, was killed in battle in 1120 near the River Shiel by Somerled, the Norse-Celtic warrior. Somerled was a pivotal figure in West Highland history. As well as inventing the hinged rudder, he commanded a fleet of over 80 ships and became the 'Ruler of the Stranger's Isles' by ousting Norse invaders and bringing stability to the Hebrides. His descendants, chiefs of Clan Donald, took the title 'Lord of the Isles' which was forfeited to the crown in 1493 and is today held by the Prince of Wales.

◀ The lochan at Glen Forslan

Ben Hiant of Ardnamurchan

Ben Hiant (528m)

Walk time **3h40** Height gain **600m**
Distance **10km** OS Map **Landranger 47**
or Explorer **390**

A compact and entertaining route with mixed terrain and some steep ascent in places. Interesting route-finding along the glen to finish.

Start at the parking place and picnic table overlooking the bay of Camus nan Geall (GR562616). Take the grassy track that leads down to the bay, passing through two stiles to reach the shore. Walk westwards along the pebbled beach, crossing the promontory of Sgeir Fhada and several smaller bays. After crossing a fence by

wooden slats after 2km, leave the beaches and climb northwards through the bracken. Follow the east side of a burn and continue steeply past an earthen scar to reach easier terrain above. Keep the knolls of Stallachan Dubha to the south and pass into the secluded bowl below the southern slopes of Ben Hiant. Climb easily northwest to reach a prominent flat area on the ridge below the rocky ramparts of the main peak. The ridge is followed without difficulty to the summit and trig point (GR537633) (2h). The cliffs are steep to the east, and care is required. Retrace your steps for about 30m to a dip on the west and then take a path that drops slowly eastwards, skirting the south side of the summit to reach easier

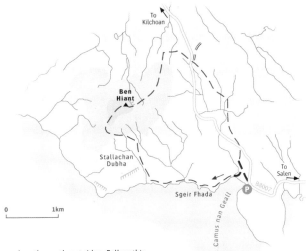

ground on the northeast ridge. Follow this around the corrie basin. The path splits after descending a short steep section about 1km from the top. Take the right fork to ascend a slight incline. This path passes a cairn and drops eastwards in fits and starts to reach the road. Cross the road, where there is a track. The remnants of an old path (to the east of the telegraph wires) wends its way southwards, contouring above the burn on the east side of the wide glen. Part of this is reinforced with old wall but most of it is hidden in the bracken and adventurous, particularly when passing a small waterfall. This route reaches the road about 800m from the start. To keep off the road until the very end, walk 80m south to a gate on the west side of the road. Go through the gate, and drop through the rough heathery field towards the bay to reach a gate by the original grassy track close to the start (3h40).

Atlantic drift

60 million years ago, mainland Scotland and North America were part of the same continental landmass. The force of rising magma from deep within the earth's crust caused the continent to split into two tectonic plates, eventually forming the basin of the Atlantic Ocean. Volcanic activity is still evident in Iceland, which lies on the join of the North American and European plates. Volcanoes and lava flows from this period are evident throughout Scotland, and can be seen most easily in Ardnamurchan, Skye and Mull.

◀ Camus nan Geall and Ben Hiant

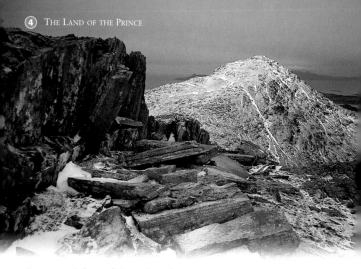

Pyramids of Lochailort

An Stac ⓒ (814m), **Rois-Bheinn** ⓒ (882m), **Sgùrr na Ba Glaise** ⓒ (874m)

Walk time **7h + detour 40 min**
Height gain **1200m** Distance **14km**
OS Map **Landranger 40**

Plenty of ascent over multiple peaks on firm terrain make this a popular walk. Easily accessed from the station at Lochailort and escapable midway.

Start at the Lochailort Inn at the junction between the A861 and A830 (GR767823). Walk northeast towards Fort William for 100m to a track that descends south by a large roadsign. Take this track past a house, and cross the River Ailort by a bridge. Turn left immediately after the bridge to follow another track east to Glenshian Lodge. Pass the main house, and thread between subsidiary buildings. The track turns south after a cowshed: follow it for a further 200m to a fork. Take the left branch to follow a grassy track past a cemetery and along the Allt an t-Sagairt. After 500m this track turns to the south and begins to climb. After a further 800m, it descends to cross the Allt a'Bhùiridh. Rather than cross the river, leave the track at its highest point and start to ascend the grassy northeast ridge of Seann Chruach. Beyond a knoll, the ridge is studded with rocks and leads to this small top. Descend south and ascend the steep northern slopes of An Stac. Low crags can be climbed or turned to reach the summit (GR763793) (3h). Descend due south over grass and the occasional steep rocky section to a bealach. [Escape: descend east into Coire a'Bhùiridh to pick up the original

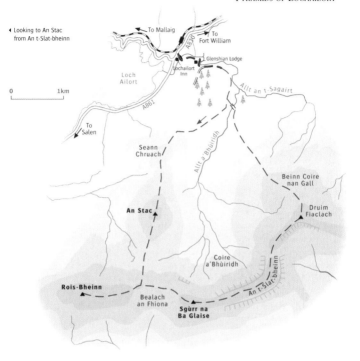

◄ Looking to An Stac from An t-Slat-bheinn

grassy track lower down.] Climb south to intercept an old fence and wall, and follow this to the east ridge of Rois-Bheinn. Detour: follow the wall to the summit and trig point. Return the same way (add 40 min).] Descend east to Bealach an Fhiona before climbing to the summit of Sgùrr na Ba Glaise. From this point, the ridge undulates east, then northeast, and the steep crags on both sides forbid an easy escape. Continue over An t-Slat-bheinn and

down to a prominent bealach. The long and undulating ridge of Druim Fiaclach, with its stepped crags above remote Glen Aladale, provides the final climb of the day. Descend steeply north from the summit to a bowl, and contour around the west flank of Beinn Coire nan Gall. Bear northwest, aiming directly for Loch Ailort and losing height easily over broad grassy slopes. Reach the Allt a'Bhùiridh and locate the bridge to retrace your steps to the start (7h).

Path of the '45

Sgùrr Ghiubhsachain ⓖ (849m)

Walk time **7h** Height gain **900m**
Distance **17km** OS Map **Landranger 40**

**Long approach to climb one high peak
with easy access from Glenfinnan
Station. Good decision-making required
for the steep and rocky descent.**

Start from the Callop Forest Trails car park
on the south side of the River Callop 2km
east of the Glenfinnan Visitor Centre
(GR924794). Follow a track south towards
the farm at Callop. After about 500m, the
track takes a sharp right turn to the farm.
Instead of following it, keep your bearing to
accompany a path between a wall and the
river. This leads easily south and starts to
gain height as the river becomes the Allt na

Cruaiche. Continue by the path as it rises
west away from the water and Caledonian
Pine, then south again to gain height. This
leads to a higher and wider glen: continue
southwest until you reach the bealach
where Cona Glen comes into view and the
path starts to descend (GR900747) (2h20).
Leave the path here, and climb slopes
northwest to Glac Gharbh before traversing
west to reach the rounded bealach towards
Leac an Fhuarain. Now tackle the southeast
face of Sgùrr Ghiubhsachain directly,
turning slabs and buttresses to reach the
summit (GR875751) (4h40). The descent of
the north ridge is a great experience, but
care should be taken as there are many
steep cliffs between here and Loch Shiel.
Descend to a subsidiary summit to the

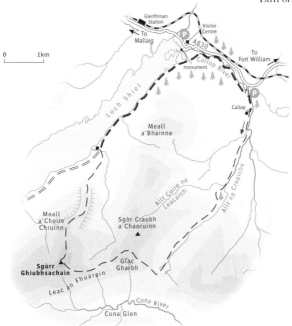

northeast, and from here take the north ridge. Any difficult sections in the upper part should be taken on the loch side, returning to the main ridge afterwards. Ascend Meall a'Choire Chruinn and continue along the spur, again turning the upper difficulties on the west. Lower down, at about 300m above the loch, there are further cliffs which are best avoided by turning east into the corrie and following grassy ramps down to a house by Loch Shiel. Follow the dirt track northeast along the loch and then close to the Callop River to the start (7h).

Raising the standard

The monument at Glenfinnan marks the spot where the Jacobite standard was raised on the 19th of August 1745. Much of the support Bonnie Prince Charlie hoped for did not materialise, however, and fewer than 1500 clansmen arrived to begin the ill-fated campaign. The clansmen that did 'come out' for the Prince paid a high price for their loyalty.

◀ The Glenfinnan Monument and Sgùrr Ghiubhsachain

A Glenfinnan circuit

Sgùrr nan Coireachan ⓜ (956m),
Sgùrr Thuilm ⓜ (963m)

Walk time 7h20 Height gain 1300m
Approach and return 40 min bike or
1h40 walk Distance 16km + 8km approach
and return OS Map Landranger 40

**Ridge walk high above a deep glen with
fine views and lots of height gain. Use
of a bike will reduce access time.**

Start in Glenfinnan, 300m west of the
visitor centre and 600m east of the railway
station at the start of a private road to the
Glenfinnan Estate (GR905808). Walk north
along the road, under McAlpine's viaduct

and for a further 3km to where the road
splits between the refurbished Glenfinnan
Estate and Corryhully Bothy. Leave bikes
here: walk times start from this point. Take
the left turn towards the house, but at the
bend about 150m take a minor track
that climbs west above the Allt a'Chaol-
ghlinne. This enters a fine glen, dominated
by the high crags of Sgùrr an Utha. The
track soon becomes a path and after about
2km stops abruptly at a cairn. Leave the
glen at this point, and climb steep slopes

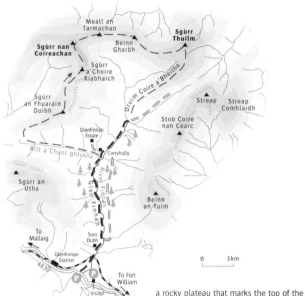

northwest to gain the west ridge of Sgùrr an Fhuarain Duibh. Follow this undulating spur east over terraces and knolls to an ill-defined top: the highest point is a hillock set to the east. Fenceposts line the route for the next 7km, making navigation easier. From the summit, trend north over rough ground to reach a bealach above the rocky Coire Carnaig. Climb northeast to pass low crags, which present no difficulties, to gain the top of Sgùrr a'Choire Riabhaich. [Escape: descend the steep southeast ridge by a good path to the glen.] Walk northwest over a rocky plateau that marks the top of the steep east-facing crags and climb to the top of Sgùrr nan Coireachan (GR903880) (3h40). From this point the ridge encounters many small knolls on a sweeping journey eastwards that gives fine views of the Rough Bounds. The easiest line is along the apex of the ridge: it is a fine 4km walk to the highest peak of the route, Sgùrr Thuilm (5h40). Descend south, following the fenceposts to join the grassy ridge of Druim Coire a'Bheithe. This guides you southwest to reach the upper glen close to a track. Follow the track to the bothy and the private road (7h20). Return to the start.

◀ Looking south along Glen Finnan above Corryhully

19

Streap

**Stob Coire nan Cearc (887m),
Streap** ⊙ **(909m)**

Walk time **7h** Height gain **1000m**
Distance **20km** OS Map **Landranger 40**

**Steep ascent to gain a high and craggy
ridge with views of the magnificent
Gleann a'Chaorainn. Good paths and
tracks assist the approach and return.**

Start in Glenfinnan, 300m west of the
visitor centre and 600m east of the railway
station at the start of a private road to the
Glenfinnan Estate (GR905808). Walk north
along the road and pass under McAlpine's
viaduct. Just past the cottage of Tom Dubh,
there is a vehicle bridge across the River
Finnan. Cross the river and take the track

on the other side to cut northwards through
the plantation. After almost 2km, the track
reaches a gate at the end of the forest.
Pass through the gate and cross the burn
by a bridge. [Variant: this point is just above
Corryhully and can be reached from the
bothy by the stepping stones or footbridge
just to the south.] Climb east up steep
grassy slopes, keeping to the left of two
burns to avoid the gulch above. This climb
is unremitting and steepens as height is
gained, eventually leading to the rocky
summit of Meall an Uillt Chaoil. Walk
northeast over rough ground to climb the
craggy knoll of Stob Coire nan Cearc. From
this point, the hulk of Streap dominates the
view. There are many steep cliffs around

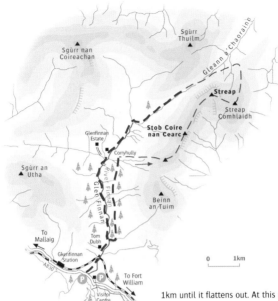

this peak and care is required. Continue more easily to the summit, gained by a narrow ridge (GR946864) (4h). Descend ESE and take the narrow ridge to Streap Comhlaidh. From this top, descend northeast to start before you can take the prominent north ridge. Follow this for about

1km until it flattens out. At this point drop easily northwest off the ridge into the upper section of the Gleann a'Chaorainn and its meandering burn. When you have reached the glen floor, turn southwest to climb gently up to the bealach between Streap and Sgùrr Thuilm. Descend by a good track on the west bank of a burn. This leads back down to Glen Finnan. Take the private road back to the start (7h).

Concrete Bob

Lanarkshire-born entrepreneur Robert McAlpine (1847-1934), founder of one of Britain's best-known building firms, earned his nickname from the innovative use of concrete in constructing his Scottish memorials which include Glenfinnan Viaduct and Borrodale Bridge. Through his sons, however, the name McAlpine became internationally known for the construction of Wembley Stadium, spiritual home of English football.

◀ The view from Streap along Gleann a'Chaorainn

Gulvain by Loch Eil

Gulvain Ⓜ (987m),
Braigh nan Uamhachan Ⓒ (765m)

Walk time **9h20** Height gain **1300m**
Distance **24km**
OS Maps Landranger 40 and 41

Long circuit of a high peak and several adventurous tops, accessed by good tracks and rough mountain terrain. There are some steep sections of ascent and descent, and navigation skills are required.

Start from the junction of the A830 with the A861 (GR959793). (Parking on the Strontian road before the railway bridge.) Take a track on the north side of the A830, and turn right before the house to cross the bridge over the Fionn Lighe. Beyond the bridge, take the first fork on the left to follow an excellent track northwards: this

rises and then falls to cross back over the river by another bridge. Pass the ruin at Wauchan and continue northeast by the river for a further 4km. Cross the Allt a'Choire Reidh by a bridge and leave the track as it turns northwest. Here, look out for the path that leads steeply northwards to tackle the broad south ridge of Gulvain, eased in the lower section by switchbacks. After a long climb, you come to a knoll: the walking eases off from here to reach a subsidiary top and trig point. Descend NNE along this high ridge, and climb to the summit of Gulvain (GR003876) (4h40). Retrace your steps back to the trig point. Descend northwest along a steep and grassy ridge: this is easier than it looks and soon leads to a flat marshy area. [Escape: descend south through boggy and difficult ground to reach the original track after

◄ Sunset on Loch Eil

2.5km.] Follow the ridge over complex terrain to the west, passing the knolls of Gualann nan Osna before climbing WSW to the summit of Braigh nan Uamhachan (GR975866) (7h). Follow the ridge southwards: an old wall snakes its way over Sròn Liath for 1.5km and fenceposts guide you over the top of Na h-Uamhachan. Cross a fence by a gate and follow the ridge southwest over undulating folds. This takes you to flatter ground, populated by young

trees, to reach another fence on the far side of the plantation just before the terrain rises again. Descend ESE, keeping close to the fence. Lower down, enter an old birch wood and continue to a high fence which is crossed by a sliding gate 150m above the ruin of Wauchan. Descend to the house and gain the original track below. Follow this back to the start (9h20).

Clan Cameron

Chiefs of the Clan Cameron take their name, Lochiel, from their original island seat of power, Eilean nan Craobh, situated in Loch Eil. In 1745 Donald Cameron, 'Gentle Lochiel', led 850 of his clansmen to Glenfinnan to join Bonnie Prince Charlie under the Stuart standard. With the rallying call, 'Sons of the hounds, come hither and get flesh', his men upheld their reputation for ferocity and courage in battle but the campaign ended with defeat on Culloden moor. Lochiel witnessed the burning of his home at Achnacarry and briefly hid out on Eilean nan Craobh before leaving for exile in France with his Prince, never to return to Lochaber.

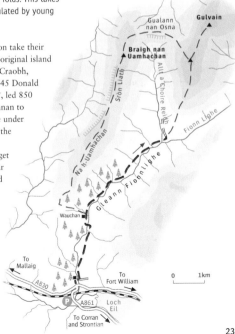

Flanked by the Lochs of Heaven (Nevis), to the south, and Hell (Hourn), to the north, Knoydart is one of Britain's most unspoilt areas, a rugged and virtually roadless peninsula accessible only by sea or on foot.

The hamlet of Inverie, nestled in a bay on the south side of the peninsula, is served by boat from Mallaig and is home to most of Knoydart's population (around 70 in total) and the most remote pub in Britain, the welcoming Old Forge Inn. The mountains of Knoydart continue eastwards to Loch Arkaig and Loch Quoich and the road-ends at Strathan and Kinlochhourn provide footpath access into Knoydart for longer expeditions.

There are three routes on the main peninsula in this section: a horseshoe of hills starting close to Inverie; a route over two

high peaks from Barrisdale; and a two-day trip over the famous mountain of Ladhar Bheinn. From Loch Arkaig there is a high traverse over many tops and a route over Sgùrr na Ciche that starts from Sourlies, at the head of Loch Nevis. In Glen Quoich the routes are shorter but still feel remote: a climb up Gairich with a return by the loch, a circuit of the twins of Gleouraich and Spidean Mialach, and a walk over two high peaks that starts close to Kinlochhourn.

The Rough Bounds of Knoydart

A Glen Kingie horseshoe

Sgùrr Cos na Breachd-laoidh ⊙ (835m),
Sgùrr nan Coireachan ⓜ (953m),
Sgùrr Mór ⓜ (1003m)

Walk time **8h40 + detour 1h20**
Height gain **1800m** Distance **22km**
OS Map **Landranger 33**

Strenuous circuit to climb several high peaks between Loch Quoich and Loch Arkaig. This route is remote and contains a river crossing.

Start at the end of the public road at the head of Loch Arkaig (GR988916). (Very limited parking.) Follow the track west to a junction after 800m. Take the upper track to walk northwest: this soon turns to dirt and follows the River Dessary. After crossing a bridge before the farm at Glendessary, leave

the track and walk northwards, close to the Allt na Fèithe. An old rocky path and grassy tracks lead through a gateway and help with the ascent. After about 1km, turn off the path and climb more steeply northwest over undulating slopes. These become rockier and lead to the top of Druim a'Chuirn. Follow the ridge westwards by a low wall and fenceposts, old boundary markers that crown the massif as far as Sgùrr na Ciche. Pass two large slabs stacked on the bealach and climb to the summit of Sgùrr Cos na Breachd-laoidh (GR948946) (3h20). Descend northwest over steep terrain to a prominent bealach. Climb An Eag by its south ridge to reach the top. [Detour: descend WNW to a bealach and follow the ridge around to the summit of Sgùrr nan Coireachan: the highest point is the nearest of three knolls. Return to An

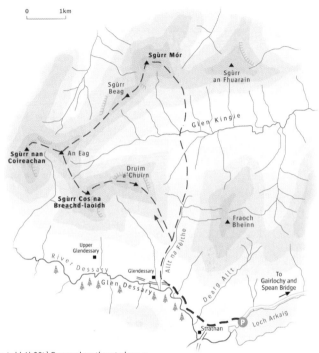

Eag (add 1h20).] Descend northeast along a fine ridge to a bealach. [Escape: find the old zigzag path that drops to the south, neatly avoiding craggy terrain to reach upper Glen Kingie.] Climb Sgùrr Beag: there is a good path that threads its way up the lower section. Descend the northeast ridge to a bealach and climb the shapely pyramid of Sgùrr Mór to its summit (GR965980) (6h). Walk east until the ridge splits, and then descend southeast towards Braigh a'Choire Bhuidhe. Rather than continue along the

ridge to Sgùrr an Fhuarain, drop southwards over the long grassy slopes that sweep right into the glen. There is no bridge across the River Kingie and you will have to ford the water at a convenient point. (In spate, it will be necessary to cross much higher.) Climb south over rough slopes to the bealach between Druim a'Chuirn and Fraoch Bheinn. Find the old path that leads back along the Allt na Fèithe, and retrace your steps back to the start (8h40).

◀ Sgùrr an Fhuarain and Sgùrr Mór from Loch Quoich

27

Loch Nevis wilderness

Ben Aden ⓖ (887m), **Sgùrr na Ciche** ⓜ
(1040m), **Garbh Chioch Mhór** ⓜ (1013m)

Walk time **7h40** + detour 40 min
Height gain **1400m** Distance **17km**
OS Map Landranger **33**
Approach Sourlies can be reached from
several directions: Along Glen Dessary
from Loch Arkaig (13km one-way); over
Màm Meadail from Inverie (12km one-way);
direct along Loch Nevis by boat or kayak

**A long approach to climb very remote
mountains. Route-finding skills are
important for the steep west ridge of
Ben Aden, and scrambling is also
required for this part of the route.**

Start from the head of Loch Nevis at the
Sourlies Bothy. Walk west around the
headland (easy when the tide is out), and

then northwards over boggy ground to
follow the River Carnoch upstream. Cross
the river at a wire bridge and turn right
along a track that soon divides, close to the
ruins of Carnoch. Take the track along the
river: this can be boggy after rain (there are
also additional tracks that keep higher).
After 3km, you reach a gorge with a
tumbling waterfall. Edge along this and
climb over boulders for about 50m. Watch
for some rusty fencing and a natural bridge
where the water is forced under a giant
rock. Cross the river and walk 30m
upstream. Climb a steep ramp on tussocky
grass to begin your ascent of Ben Aden.
This breaches all of the crags in the lower
section. Continue over easier terrain
towards the imposing west ridge. The spur
steepens as you progress, although grassy

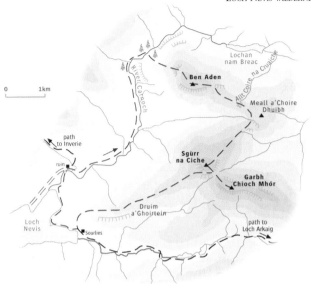

runnels can be followed for most of the way until there is a slight break before a steep band of broken crags. A line in the centre is the easiest: it requires good scrambling and a cool nerve to find a twisting way through the quartz slabs to easy ground above. Continue to the summit of Ben Aden (GR899986) (4h). Descend by the east ridge for about 400m. Leave this by a series of sloping terraces that lead you down the south side to complex ground. Walk ESE over slabs to reach three lochans. Rather than climb Meall a'Choire Dhuibh, which has steep rocky ramparts, contour around the upper corrie and then join the northeast ridge of Sgùrr na Ciche. This can be followed without any difficulty to the

summit (GR902967) (6h20). Descend south and then southeast from the top to gain a bealach with a low wall. [Detour: climb Garbh Chioch Mhór, passing low crags with a couple of rock steps to reach the summit. Return to the bealach (add 40 min).] Begin a rising traverse westwards that cuts across the south face of Sgùrr na Ciche. This reaches Druim a'Ghoirtein, the west ridge, below its steepest section. Walk down the ridge: boggier reaches interperse with firmer terrain and it commands fine views of Loch Nevis. When you are close to sea level and have passed the steep slabs on the south side of the spur, descend directly to the bothy for a welcome brew (7h40).

◄ Garbh Chioch Mhór from Sgùrr nan Coireachan

29

Gleann Meadail circuit

Meall Buidhe Ⓜ(946m),
Beinn Bhuidhe Ⓒ(855m)

Walk time **9h20** Height gain **1300m**
Distance **24km** OS Map Landranger 33
Access Inverie is reached from Mallaig
by ferry.

**Good access tracks to climb multiple
peaks in rough terrain above a less
visited glen. Care and good decision-
making is required for the steep
sections in descent.**

Start at Inverie Pier (GR766000). Take the
road leading southeast from the village and
watch for a track on the left after 800m,
signposted for Kinlochhourn. Follow this
track as it climbs through the trees. At

Corry, reached after 500m, go through the
gate ahead and follow the track eastwards,
passing beneath Brocket's Monument to
reach a junction and second signpost. Take
the right fork (south) to cross the Inverie
River. This track continues eastwards past
the private Druim Bothy and into the
hidden Gleann Meadail. Cross the bridge to
the north side of the glen. Rather than
follow the path along the glen, climb north
up steep grassy slopes to the right of
broken, tree-lined crags to gain the fine
spur of Druim Righeanaich. Continue more
easily along the ridge to the top of An t-
Uiriollach. A short drop to a bealach gives
access to the final slopes of Meall Buidhe
(GR849989) (4h20). Continue to the east

summit and make a southeast descent towards Sgùrr Sgeithe. Soon after passing a hollow which feeds a burn (about 300m from the east summit) descend south off the ridge, switching steeply between low crags to reach a bealach above Màm Meadail. [Escape: descend west through Gleann Meadail by a good path.] Follow undulating ground to climb Meall Bhasiter, with one cairn on its top and another beyond. Continue west along the ridge, meeting small crags and pools before dropping to Màm Uchd. Beinn Bhuidhe comes next. The lower east top has a steep face to negotiate but can be climbed via its southern aspect, zigzagging between

buttresses. The west top presents no difficulties (GR822967) (6h40). Descend west to Bealach Buidhe before climbing the last peak of Sgùrr Coire nan Gobhar. Drop north from the crinkled top, staying shy of cliffs to the east. This descent is steep in a couple of places and arrives close to a lochan. Climb northwards to Sgùrr nan Feadan and take its east ridge towards Gleann Meadail. Lower down, the ridge forks and steepens: take a line between the two noses to reach a plantation fence. Keep this on your left as you cross boggy ground to the waterfall. Follow the river downstream to the bridge, and retrace your steps to Inverie (9h20).

Lord Brocket

A vociferous admirer of Hitler, the notorious Lord Brocket bought the Knoydart estate in the 1930s to use as his personal playground. Somehow, his political loyalties did not deter the government from backing him when seven local men staged a land raid on his estate after the war. Heroes in the battle for land rights in the Highlands, a memorial in Inverie commemorates their stand.

◀ Loch an Dubh-Lochain from Màm Barrisdale

The Jewel of Knoydart

Ladhar Bheinn ⑩ (1020m)

Walk time **10h20** Height gain **1500m**
Distance **29km** OS Map Landranger 33
Access Inverie is reached by ferry from
Mallaig. Barrisdale can be reached on foot
from Kinlochhourn (10km one-way).

**A remote gem in this wild land,
accessed by good paths and a trek
along a fine ridge with slight exposure
above deep corries. A stopover at
Barrisdale makes it an easier
two-day trek.**

Start at Inverie Pier
(GR766000). Take the

road southeast from the village and watch
for a track on the left after 800m,
signposted for Kinlochhourn. Follow this
track as it climbs through the trees. At
Corry, reached after 500m, pass through the
gate ahead and follow the track east, then
northeast into Gleann an Dubh-Lochain.
Keep to the track to the end of Loch an
Dubh-Lochain, after which it diminishes to a
path. Now begin the long steady climb to
the bealach at Màm Barrisdale. Drop down
the other side on a similar path to reach
the bothy at Barrisdale, just over the
river (GR872043) (4h). On the
west bank of the river,

follow a path which trends northwest across the grassy flatlands towards the lower part of the Creag Bheithe ridge. Start to climb in zigzags over the snout of the ridge. The path then levels out, begins to enter birch woodland and turns a corner into a magnificent glen, dominated by Ladhar Bheinn and the four buttresses of Coire Dhorrcail. Follow the path as it snakes high above the ravine to arrive at flatter ground. Cross the Allt Coire Dhorrcail and, rather than continue into the corrie, forge directly northwest up grassy slopes to gain the apex of the complex north ridge of Druim a'Choire Odhair. Ascend the ridge southwest along a good path, passing boulders and crags. Climb steeply to the top of Stob a'Choire Odhair, and drop a short way beyond, with a few exposed moves on the

ridge between the corries. The summit of Ladhar Bheinn is a short climb beyond (GR823040) (7h40). Walk WNW along the level top to the trig point. Begin a gradual descent along the west ridge over firm terrain, dropping more steeply to reach An Diollaid. Descend southwest from here over the grassy slopes of Coire Garbh, aiming for the south corner of the nearest triangular plantation. This is never difficult, although it can get boggy. Join the path along the Allt Coire Torr an Asgaill and follow this past the ruin of Folach to a bridge. Cross to the south side of the burn and take the gravel track after 100m. Follow this along the river and then up through a second plantation to reach another gravel track after 3km. Turn left to head south into Inverie (10h20).

◀ Stob a'Choire Odhair from Ladhar Bheinn

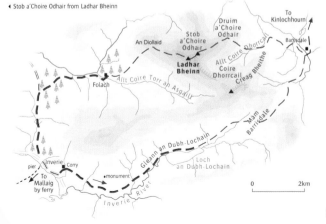

33

Twins of Barrisdale

Luinne Bheinn Ⓜ (939m),
Sgùrr a'Choire-bheithe Ⓒ (913m)

Walk time **8h20** Height gain **1400m**
Distance **22km** OS Map Landranger 33
Approach **Barrisdale** has a bothy,
bunkhouse and camping area. It can be
accessed from several directions: along
Loch Hourn from Kinlochhourn (10km one-
way); along Gleann an Dubh-Lochain from
Inverie (13km one-way); direct across Loch
Hourn by boat from Corran

**A high craggy route over two peaks
whose many corries and ridges are
made easier with good scrambling skills.**

   Start from the bothy in Barrisdale
(GR872043). Walk south over the bridge
past the bunkhouse and take the path that
rises steadily to the bealach of Màm
Barrisdale. Leave the path here, and climb

southeast. Keep to the main ridge, climbing
steeply at first to gain Bachd Mhic an
Tosaich where the terrain eases over bumps
and folds. It steepens again by a delta of
scree and, after more rocky knolls, reaches
the summit of Luinne Bheinn with its many
tops (GR869008) (3h). Follow the high
ground around Coire Glas and take the east
ridge which drops through entertaining
boulders and crags to reach the bealach at
Màm Unndalain. [Escape: take the path
northwest along Gleann Unndalain to
Barrisdale.] Climb northwards over the steep
ground at the southern flanks of Sgùrr
a'Choire-bheithe, its boulders flecked with
silver mica. Some good decision-making is
required to find an easy way through the
upper crags. Once on the main ridge, the
top is easily gained. Descend ESE to follow
the less-walked ridge of Druim Chòsaidh.

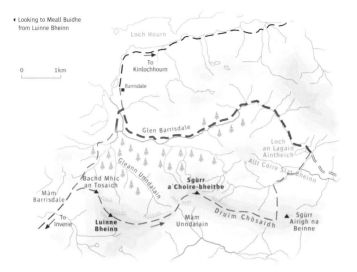

◀ Looking to Meall Buidhe
from Luinne Bheinn

This spur has two obvious towers that are slightly exposed and require care on descent. These difficulties are short-lived, however, and lead to undulating ground with a few small knolls. Follow the ridge for 1km beyond the towers until the ground rises again at Sgùrr Airigh na Beinne. At this point, it is easy to descend north to the floor of the glen. Follow the burn

downstream for about 500m. Then turn north, passing west of a knoll and over gnarled tree roots. A boggy stretch takes you to an excellent grassy track by the secluded Loch an Lagain Aintheich. The track leads gently northwest and then west through a remote country of meadow, old forest and cascades to reach Barrisdale (8h20).

The Clearances of Knoydart

After Culloden, there was an extensive period of emigration to Canada from Knoydart but in 1846 there were still at least 600 residents on the peninsula. The potato blight and reduced herring stocks in Loch Nevis had a disastrous effect and led to further exodus. In the 1850s, Josephine MacDonell, widow of the clan chief, felt she had little option but to offer her tenants assisted emigration. She sold the estate soon after, and realised a better price now that it was clear for sheep.

Between Quoich and Hourn

Sgùrr Thionail (906m),
Sgùrr a'Mhaoraich Ⓜ (1027m)

Walk time **5h20** Height gain **1200m**
Distance **12km** OS Map **Landranger 33**

Good paths access two rocky peaks on a winding ridge beyond the end of Glen Quoich by Kinlochhourn. Care is required on the intricate and steep descent.

Start 1km south of Kinlochhourn by the foot of Loch Coire Shubh, where a sign marks a right of way to Shiel Bridge (GR958055). (Additional parking in Kinlochhourn.) Walk east along the track and cross the burn by the stepping stones. Follow the track around a knoll and then northwards to gain steady height. This continues northeast beneath pylons before coming to a junction by a burn: take the upper branch and continue above the Allt Coire Sgoireadail. Higher up, where the glen widens, the track fades to a grassy path which is sometimes harder to follow. Begin a steeper climb, keeping close to the cascading burn and a series of fenceposts, to a cairn on a knobbly bealach. Leave the path at the cairn, and climb east to discover Loch Bealach Coire Sgoireadail. Continue east over rough ground for 500m. Ignore a path that descends northwards, and climb steep ground to quickly gain the north ridge of Sgùrr Thionail. This is followed more easily over grass and past low crags. A subtle rocky fin marks the halfway point,

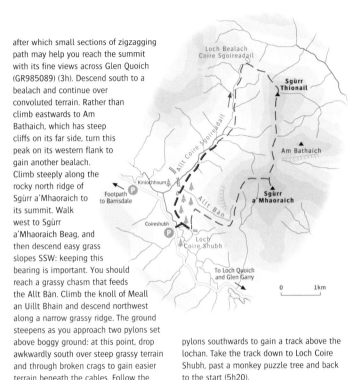

after which small sections of zigzagging path may help you reach the summit with its fine views across Glen Quoich (GR985089) (3h). Descend south to a bealach and continue over convoluted terrain. Rather than climb eastwards to Am Bathaich, which has steep cliffs on its far side, turn this peak on its western flank to gain another bealach. Climb steeply along the rocky north ridge of Sgùrr a'Mhaoraich to its summit. Walk west to Sgùrr a'Mhaoraich Beag, and then descend easy grass slopes SSW: keeping this bearing is important. You should reach a grassy chasm that feeds the Allt Bàn. Climb the knoll of Meall an Uillt Bhain and descend northwest along a narrow grassy ridge. The ground steepens as you approach two pylons set above boggy ground: at this point, drop awkwardly south over steep grassy terrain and through broken crags to gain easier terrain beneath the cables. Follow the

pylons southwards to gain a track above the lochan. Take the track down to Loch Coire Shubh, past a monkey puzzle tree and back to the start (5h20).

The Old Forge

Certified by the Guinness Book of Records as Britain's most remote pub, The Old Forge Inn at Inverie is 21 miles from Kinlochhourn through some of the roughest terrain in the Highlands. It is more commonly reached by ferry from Mallaig, although moorings are also available. With award-winning ales, wild venison and a legendary seafood platter, it is well worth a visit, however you get there. Dress code: waterproofs and midge cream.

◄ Glen Quoich and Spidean Meallach from Sgùrr a'Mhaoraich

Stalking Spidean Mialach

Gleouraich  (1035m),
Spidean Mialach ⓜ (996m)

Walk time **5h20** Height gain **1200m**
Distance **12km** OS Map **Landranger 33**

An exposed ridge taking in two high peaks and reached by stalkers' paths. This route requires good mountain judgement in winter conditions.

Start at the promontory below the weather station, 3km west of the dam at the head of Loch Quoich (GR044018). (Parking available.) Walk northwest along the road above the site of the now submerged Quoich Lodge. Once you have crossed a bridge after 2km, watch for a path through the rhododendrons: the botanical legacy of the former estate. This path runs alongside the Allt Coire Peitireach and climbs steeply in zigzags towards the prominent ridge of Sròn a'Chuilin. Follow the ridge northwards as its western flanks become rockier and more exposed. The ridge flattens out to give a final steep climb northeast to the summit of Gleouraich (GR040053) (3h). Care should be taken along the length of this exposed ridge to Spidean Mialach. In winter conditions, the

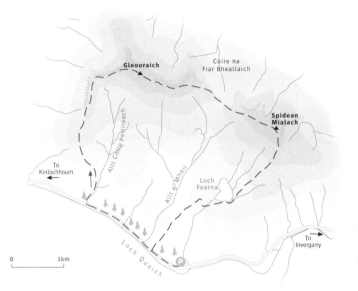

cornice may overhang considerably. Take the main ridge ESE to an intermediary summit before a long and steep descent to the bealach above Coire Dubh. Follow the crest of the ridge to the summit of Spidean Mialach and its slender northern spurs (GR066043) (4h20). Descend easily southwest from the top over easy slopes of heather and scree, aiming for the east side of Loch Fearna. Skirt the loch to its south bank and cross the outlet burn. Continue southwest along a vague ridge, diverging slowly from the burn. Descend southwest over uneven slopes, keeping the radio masts just to the left, to reach the road and the start (5h20).

Chasing the deer

Red deer feed for 10 to 13 hours a day, divided into many sessions and interspersed with rumination and rest. Procreation takes up the remainder of their time. In late summer, groups of stags split up to search out rutting grounds where the hinds roam free. Stags then attach themselves to hind groups, and will defend their 'harems' from rivals. During confrontation, stags will roar first, fight second – a procedure that prevents excessive injury.

◄ Stags by Loch Quoich

Queen of Loch Quoich

Gairich (M) (919m)

Walk time **5h40** Height gain **800m**
Distance **15km** OS Map **Landranger 33**

**A single peak at the head of Glen Garry
reached over rough terrain with one
steep climb. The route descends direct
to Loch Quoich by the north ridge.**

Start from the dam at the foot of Loch
Quoich (GR070025). Walk along the top of
the dam and take a path which wanders
south across undulating ground. Pass
Lochan an Fhigheadair to reach a more
prominent path and gate at the entrance to
a large plantation. From this point, climb
steeply west following the line of the fence.
This soon gains an excellent path that
winds its way up Druim na Geid Salaich and
gains the small plateau of Bac nam Fòid.
Drop gently west to a boggy area and then

Rainy days

With an annual average rainfall in its catchment area of 3170mm, Loch Quoich is an
important storage reservoir. At its eastern end is the largest rockfill dam in Scotland: some
320m long, 38m high with a base width of 90m. Its waters power the Quoich station on
the banks of the River Garry.

▼ Gairich and Loch Quoich

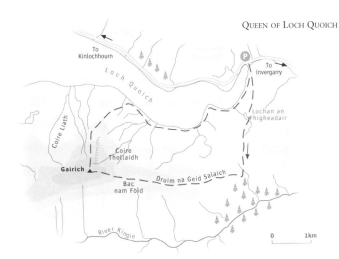

begin a steep ascent, turning low buttresses to reach the summit of Gairich (GR025995) (3h20). Descend due north along a broad ridge, avoiding the temptation to bear eastwards as there are steep cliffs in Coire Thollaidh. Once you get close to Loch Quoich and the terrain to the east eases, leave the ridge and bear northeast to limit the lochside walking. The water's edge can then be followed eastwards. This return may involve fording several burns, depending on the weather. Return to the dam (5h40).

Twisting roads lead westwards from the Great Glen at Invergarry and Invermoriston and join at the dammed Loch Cluanie to form the ancient Road to the Isles.

The loch is set in fine mountain country where long ridges descend in sweeping curves from summit to glen. At its head lies the Cluanie Inn, the only habitation for many miles. Continuing west takes you into Glen Shiel, its narrow defile enclosed by steep buttresses on both sides: spurs that provide some of the best ridge walking in the country. Beyond lies the sea to Skye.

Two routes in this section overlook Loch Lochy, southwest of Invergarry: the first involves varied terrain and starts from the road to Loch Arkaig; a harder walk starts from Laggan Locks. A demanding route starts by Moriston Bridge to climb a long horseshoe in the Ceannacroc Forest. Three routes start at the Cluanie Inn: two walks of contrasting length climb the hills to the

north, and these can be varied to suit stamina. The third route from the inn walks the famous South Shiel Ridge, involving many peaks. The western part of this ridge makes a compact route, starting from an historic battle site in Glen Shiel. A final route gives a test of uphill stamina on a spur that rises straight from the glen.

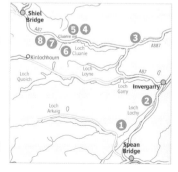

The Great Glen to Glen Shiel

Achnacarry manoeuvres

Meall na Tanga (m)(917m),
Meall Coire Lochain (906m)

Walk time **6h20** Height gain **1000m**
Distance **19km** OS Map **Landranger 34**

Two peaks with finely sculpted corries reached by good access paths and tracks that make for a long approach. This route involves one river crossing and good navigation to return.

Start from the waterfalls of Eas Chia-aig, close to the foot of Loch Arkaig (GR177888). From the car park take the path that climbs alongside the falls, the zigzag ascent through the trees accompanied by the thunderous sound of water. This path soon meets a dirt track. Follow this track northwards as it gains gradual height through the forest before losing altitude as it narrows to a path. At a fence and stile, the path leads into open country. Cross the stile and continue above the Abhainn Chia-aig, crossing to the other side of the river at a wooden bridge and then heading northeast around Meall an Tagraidh. The path follows a line of fenceposts to the ruin of Fedden (GR201941) (2h20). From here, bear due east across the burn and wide glen: on the far side, a steep incline leads to another good path. Follow this east up to Càm Bhealach. Climb south by a path from the

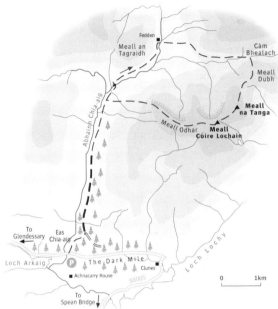

bealach to a plateau just west of Meall Dubh, then ascend the steep north ridge of Meall na Tanga and follow this to the summit (GR220925) (4h20). Drop southwest along the narrow arête between two great corries, and climb Meall Coire Lochain beyond. (This section is less steep and exposed than it looks.) Contour westwards along the curving summit ridge of Meall Odhar for 1km. Descend westwards over easy grass slopes, keeping to the north side of a gully. This bearing leads directly down to the edge of the plantation. Follow the path and track through the trees and back to the falls (6h20).

Castle Commando

Between Loch Lochy and Loch Arkaig stretches the Dark Mile, a tree-lined avenue which hides Achnacarry House, the ancestral seat of the Camerons of Lochiel and training base for Commando units in the Second World War. Known locally as Castle Commando, more than 25,000 crack troops gained basic training here. The monument designed by Scott Sutherland near Spean Bridge commemorates those who died in action.

◀ The Caledonian Canal, Gairlochy at the foot of Loch Lochy

45

Ben Tee from Laggan Locks

Ben Tee ⊙ (901m),
Sròn a'Choire Ghairbh ⊚ (935m)

Walk time **7h** Height gain **1400m**
Distance **18km** OS Map **Landranger 34**

Great horseshoe of peaks with plenty of ascent, reached from the Caledonian Canal. This route involves some tough ground and a steep descent, with an intricate return requiring sound navigation skills.

Start at Laggan Locks at the north end of Loch Lochy, accessed from the A82 (GR286963). Cross to the west side of the Caledonian Canal, and take the minor road past several holiday cabins to reach a road

along the west side of Loch Lochy. Follow this southwest towards the farm at Kilfinnan. Just before reaching a bridge at the farm, leave the road and follow a footpath signposted for Tomdoun. Climb steeply northwards through the heather: the path then levels out above the ravine of Kilfinnan Burn. Contour above the river to the west to reach a gate. Beyond the gate, cross westwards over open and boggy country for 1km to gain gradual height. Bear northwest before entering Coire Buidhe in order to gain the broad east ridge of Ben Tee. Follow this to the summit (GR241972) (3h20). Drop WSW down steep slopes of heather and scree to reach the

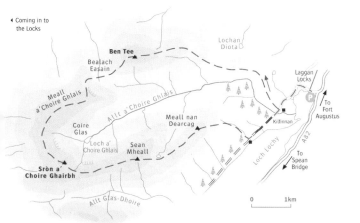

prominent Bealach Easain. Cross the flats and climb west up a wide grassy gully, keeping steep broken crags to your left. This joins a ridge running to the east end of Meall a'Choire Ghlais, with its fine ridge high above a corrie. Follow the ridge WSW and then southwards to the summit of Sròn a'Choire Ghairbh (GR222945) (5h). Descend southeast and climb to a second top: from here, the ridge narrows as it runs ENE to a small bealach. Climb Sean Mheall and drop east to a lochan. Continue along the increasingly complex ridge towards Meall

nan Dearcag, and climb to the summit. Descend eastwards, passing bands of broken cliff and crossing awkward heather to reach a fence that contours around the hill. Locate a stile at an intersection with another fence, about 1km from the farm. Climb over the stile into a steep field and head straight down towards more holiday cabins, keeping just right of a burn. A gate gives access to a gravel track opposite the cabins. Walk northeast along the track to the farm at Kilfinnan, and retrace your steps to the start (7h).

The Great Glen Way

The Great Glen Way is Scotland's fourth waymarked National Long Distance Walking Route and links Fort William with Inverness along the Great Glen Fault. The route is 73 miles (118km) long and closely follows the line of the Caledonian Canal, a much used shipping link in the 19th and earlier 20th centuries allowing trade to avoid the Pentland Firth and the French privateers during the Napoleonic Wars.

Glenmoriston getaway

Sail Chaorainn Ⓜ (1002m),
Sgùrr nan Conbhairean Ⓜ (1109m),
Carn Ghluasaid Ⓜ (957m)

Walk time **9h** Height gain **1300m**
Distance **27km** OS Map **Landranger 34**

High peaks and remote corries make for a strenuous but rewarding day out. This route involves a long approach by a sandy track unsuitable for biking.

Start off the A887 at a track and sign for the Ceannacroc Power Station, 1.5km east of the A87/A887 junction at Moriston Bridge (GR225105). (Several parking places.)

Take the private tarmac road northwards along the River Moriston to the whitewashed buildings of Ceannacroc Lodge. Continue north through a gate and along a track by the River Doe, climbing gently. Soon, the track levels out: follow it northwest for 7km to a bridge at the confluence of two burns and a ramshackle metal bothy beyond (GR175147). From the back of the bothy, follow a sunken path to climb the east ridge of An Reithe. Where the path stops abruptly at a boulder, continue to make the easy ascent, passing one false summit to reach the rocky top.

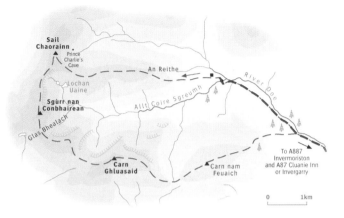

Descend west to a bealach and climb Carn a'Mhadaidh-ruaidh. A short, steep section of slabs and grass leads to the high plateau of Sail Chaorainn: the main summit lies to the north (GR133155) (4h40). From the top, double back south for 300m and pick up a path bearing southwest to a bealach. Climb south along a curving ridge to gain the summit of Sgùrr nan Conbhairean with its steep eastern cliffs. Descend southwards to Glas Bhealach. Follow the ridge eastwards over a small knoll and to the top of Carn Ghluasaid: this peak gives great views into the corries below and back to Sgùrr nan Conbhairean. Continue east, losing height gently: after 1km a cairn marks the top of Bachd na Fribheach. This is a tricky ridge in descent: instead, drop southeast over Creag Dubh and down to a bealach. Climb undulating ground east to the rocky terraces at the top of Carn nam Feuaich. Descend gently ENE over firm ground to Sròn Badan nam Meann. From here, the terrain steepens but there are no difficulties. Aim for a bend in the River Doe and descend to a thin band of trees. This leaves only a short boggy stretch to reach the original track. Return to the start (9h).

H V Morton

'Fifteen miles of beauty lie between hills. They are called Glenmoriston. There is dark Loch Cluanie, there are scraggy deer forests, then the glen seems suddenly to peal with laughter as the road dives into thick birch woods alive with rabbits. What a perfect glen this is.' Author of the classic *In Search of Scotland*, H V Morton was the world's first great travel writer whose highly influential books sold in their millions in the 1930s, '40s and '50s. He died in Africa in 1979, aged 87.

◀ Sgùrr nan Conbhairean from the east

A short from the Cluanie

Am Bathach ⊙ (798m)

Walk time **3h40** Height gain **600m**
Distance **9km** OS Map **Landranger 33**

**Compact route to climb one peak with a
steep descent into the glen. This route
can be extended to include Ciste Dhubh.**

Start at a parking area by a plantation,
1km east of the Cluanie Inn (GR086120).
Walk to the western tip of the plantation
where there is an old gate. Pass through the

gate, and follow a good gravel path
northwest along the forest. The path soon
turns to cross the flats and keeps close to
the Allt a'Caorainn Bhig through occasional
boggy patches. Continue along the glen:
further up, the path climbs to gain the
quaggy Bealach a'Choinich, which sits
perfectly between three high peaks. Walk
southeast from the bealach and climb
grassy slopes to the summit of Am Bathach
(GR073143) (2h40). The high ridge is sharp-

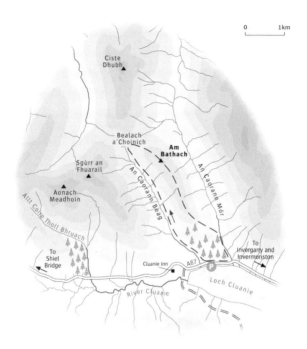

sided for 1.5km but never exposed as it climbs several knolls. A path drops southeast, steeply at first, and then follows the eastern side of the plantation to the road at a gate (3h40). [Variant: climb Ciste Dhubh from Bealach a'Choinich, and return along An Caorann Mór. This is described in the next route: A Cluanie double.]

Cluanie Inn

The Cluanie Inn at the west end of Loch Cluanie is a good base from which to explore the surrounding hills (route cards can be posted on the noticeboard). The original buildings on the site of the present inn were probably used by officers during the construction of the military road from Fort Augustus to Glenelg and Bernera Barracks. This was completed in the late 18th century by General Caulfield, General Wade's successor, and some of the original route can still be seen from higher ground.

◄ Am Bathach and the hills of Glen Shiel from A'Chralaig

A Cluanie double

Aonach Meadhoin ⓜ (1001m),
Ciste Dhubh ⓜ (929m)

Walk time **7h** Height gain **1200m**
Distance **17km** OS Map **Landranger 33**

Great route to climb two high peaks with fine views of the mountains of Kintail. There are some steep sections of ascent and descent on rocky ridges and an easy return through a wide glen.

Start at the Cluanie Inn (GR076117). Walk southwest along the A87 for 200m to a layby on the north side. Take a track from here that leads parallel to the road and just to the right of a fence. This is the Old Military Road, now barely more then a rough path: follow it past a green shed and some old duns. The army road disintegrates

further on, but continue west towards the plantation where a good path can be found near the Allt Coire Tholl Bhruach. Follow this northwards along the burn. Soon after passing a waterfall from Coire na Cadha, leave the path which now veers westwards and instead head due north up a steep grassy spur, the blunt south ridge of Aonach Meadhoin. It is a tough climb to reach the summit directly (GR049138) (3h). Descend steeply ENE along the fine arête, and then climb easily to the summit of Sgùrr an Fhuarail. Drop down the north ridge, steeply at first, to the claggy Bealach a'Choinich, the meeting point of three mountains. [Escape: descend southeast into An Caorann Beag and follow a good path on the east side of the burn. This brings you out on the

52

◄ Sgùrr na Ciste Duibhe and The Cuillin from Aonach Meadhoin

road at the west end of a plantation, 1km east of the Cluanie Inn.] Walk north over the bealach to begin a steep climb north. This soon relents and leads to a ridge with two rocky bumps. The first of these is best taken on the west side, the second climbed directly. A path leads along the narrow crest to the summit of Ciste Dhubh. Descend ENE from the top, passing a notch, and drop steeply down the east

ridge. Lower down, this relents and it is easier to drop southeast off the ridge to follow the burns down to the watershed between Glen Affric and Loch Cluanie. Cross the boggy reaches to the other side of the glen, and find a poor path that takes you south. After 1km, this becomes a good track that leads to the road. Walk west along the road for 1.5km to reward yourself with a dram (7h).

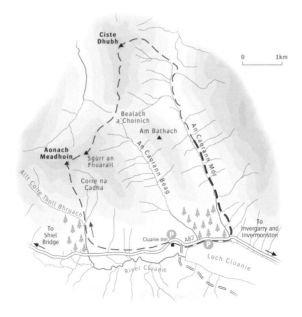

On the South Shiel Ridge

Creag a'Mhaim ⓜ (947m), **Druim Shionnach** ⓜ (987m), **Aonach air Chrith** ⓜ (1021m), **Maol Chinn-dearg** ⓜ (981m), **Sgùrr an Doire Leathain** ⓜ (1010m)

Walk time 7h + detour 40 min
Height gain 1100m Distance 19km
OS Map Landranger 33

Steep climb to gain a great ridge which then keeps its height. This walk can be extended by combining it with the next circuit: South Shiel Ridge to the west.

Start at the Cluanie Inn (GR076117). Walk east on the main road for about 300m, and turn onto a track that crosses the head of Loch Cluanie. This was the old road to Fort William before the damming of Loch Loyne. Walk along the track for about 3km, gaining height steadily, until you cross a bridge. Leave the road at this point and follow the Allt Guibhais upstream through the heather into the Coirean an Eich Bhric. Leave the corrie and climb the north ridge to the summit of Creag a'Mhaim (3h). The hard work is complete: height is now maintained for the rest of the route. Descend northwest to a bealach and climb Druim Shionnach along a narrowing ridge.

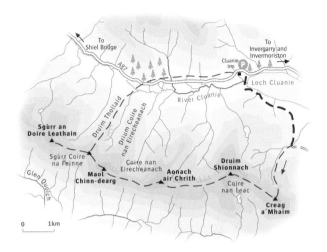

This peak is left by gentle slopes: the spur involves many small knolls overlooking the organ pipes of the northern corries. A short push gains the top of Aonach air Chrith (GR051083) (4h40). Continue west on a slow descent before climbing two knolls over which a path snakes incessantly to keep to the highest ground. This leads easily to the summit of Maol Chinn-dearg. The ridge curves northwest from here: follow it for 500m and climb to the knoll of Sgùrr Coire na Feinne. [Detour: descend a short way WNW to a prominent bealach, and then begin an easy climb to the top of Sgùrr an Doire Leathain. Return to Sgùrr Coire na Feinne (add 40 min) or continue to the end of the ridge, following part of the next route: South Shiel Ridge to the west.] Descend Druim Thollaid, the northeast ridge, with ease. This drops in waves with some low crags that line the eastern corrie. Trend eastwards as you approach the floor of the glen. Cross the burn, and climb up to the road at a large layby. Walk 900m east along the road to a bridge over the Allt Coire Tholl Bruach at the end of the plantation. To avoid more road walking, climb north on a track on the east side of the burn to reach a dun after 150m. Head east from here and maintain this course. The Old Military Road lies at this level and improves as you walk. Later it is joined by a fence, and leads after 2km to the road near the Cluanie Inn (7h).

◀ The ridge from the south

South Shiel Ridge to the west

Sgùrr an Lochain (1004m),
Creag nan Damh (918m)

Walk time **5h20** Height gain **1400m**
Distance **9km** OS Map **Landranger 33**

**Steep route to climb high peaks. This
can be combined with the previous
route (On the South Shiel Ridge) for a
longer trek. Keen navigation skills are a
must for this difficult terrain.**

Start by the two bridges over the River
Shiel (GR991132). About 200m west of the

modern roadbridge, opposite a large parking
bay, a track leads into the trees. Follow it
for about 400m until it ends. Now walk
eastwards to pick up a rough path that
climbs to level ground above the trees.
Here, there is a fence with a gateway to a
good path. Follow the path as it zigzags to
gain height above the burn. Soon, this

descends to a bridge over pools and cascades. Cross the bridge and immediately begin to climb diagonally southwards over the clumpy grass of Druim a'Choire Reidh. Pass right of a band of slabs, and climb terraces and steep grass to a knoll. An even steeper section has a rocky spur that leads to undulating terrain above. A final climb takes you onto the much easier upper spur that can be followed southwards to reach the top of Sgùrr Beag. Descend southeast to a bealach before climbing to the summit of Sgùrr an Lochain (GR006104) (3h20). Return

to Sgùrr Beag and continue gently west to a wide bealach. This gives an easy start to Creag nan Damh, which then steepens before the top. Descend by the northeast ridge. After about 300m, this forks: a seemingly easier eastern spur leads into the hanging corrie and harder terrain. Instead, descend the blunt northeast ridge: this is steep but holds no surprises. Lower down, zigzag through sharp crags and drop into the lower corrie. Walk downstream to find the original path and follow this back to the start (5h20).

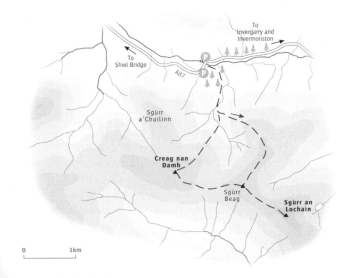

The Whelk

Faochag ⓖ (909m),
Sgùrr na Sgine ⓜ (946m)

Walk time **4h40** Height gain **9km**
Distance **1000m** OS Map **Landranger 33**

Relatively short route with a long and rewarding initial climb that makes for a great workout.

Start from the straight stretch of road by a strip of plantation, 7km southeast of Shiel Bridge (GR972139). Walk through a gate on the south side and follow a path signposted for Kinlochhourn, Tomdoun and Loch Quoich. After about 400m, cross the Allt Coire Mhàlagain and head up to a stile opposite the ford to access the northeast ridge of Faochag (the Whelk). Cross the stile over the deer fence, and climb southwest by a good path. Cross another stile and continue the ascent. The climbing rarely relents, becoming ever steeper on the approach to the summit (GR954124) (2h20). The ridge now undulates westwards to a shallow bealach. Bear south to ascend Sgùrr na Sgine, taking a circuitous route through boulders and rocks to its summit ridge: the true top lies at the far southeastern end (GR946114) (3h20). The cliffs to the east are steep, so return northwest for 200m to a hollow on the ridge just before the first top. Descend north by a steep grassy gully that leads to a large level ramp with slabs and

standing water. This ramp trends eastwards, guiding you down, never with difficulty, towards the corrie below. Follow the burn on its west bank through this flat, grassy basin: after it drops to join a tributary from the south, the path that descends from Bealach Duibh Leac can be joined. Take this path back to the start (4h40).

Spaniards in the heather

In 1719 a battle was fought at Shiel Bridge between a government army and a small Jacobite force which included around 300 white-coated Spanish troops. The original force was some 5000 strong but only two frigates made it to land at Loch Alsh; others turned back in stormy weather or were lost. Further lack of support from the Lowlands put the Jacobites at a disadvantage in the battle and they disbanded after a short fight. Most of the Spaniards survived, however, and were soon repatriated. Above the bridge on the north side, Sgùrr nan Spainteach, Peak of the Spaniards, is named in their honour.

◀ Faochag and the Saddle from the site of the 1719 Battle of Glenshiel

Kintail means 'head of two seas' in Gaelic and refers to the juncture of Loch Duich and Loch Long. They meet at Eilean Donan, an important strategic point in past centuries with what is probably the most photographed castle in Scotland.

Kintail contains some of the highest peaks in the West Highlands, including the magnificent Five Sisters, viewed most dramatically from the road to Glenelg. This ridge and several other massifs are owned by the National Trust for Scotland, which ensures perpetual access to the hills for everyone.

The routes in this section include an unconventional circuit of the exposed Forcan ridge from Shiel Bridge, a long approach from the north to climb Beinn Sgritheall and a shorter walk on mixed terrain by the shores of Loch Hourn. Two walks begin at the National Trust for Scotland centre at Morvich: an extended

traverse of the Five Sisters and a hard trek over the Beinn Fhada massif. Two routes start at the head of Loch Long: a circuit of the distant hills overlooking Loch Mullardoch (best reached by mountain bike) and a shorter walk on Ben Killilan. The final route involves an arduous bike approach from Loch Carron to climb the remote peak of Lurg Mhór.

Peaks of Kintail

Forcan Ridge and the Saddle

The Saddle ⓜ (1010m)

Walk time **7h40** Height gain **1000m**
Distance **16km** OS Map **Landranger 33**

A strenuous route with a river crossing and mandatory scrambling. Climbing skills or a rope will be useful. This route is especially tricky in winter conditions.

Start from Shiel Bridge campsite and garage (GR937186). Walk south through the campsite, and take the path that zigzags up into the hidden glen beyond. Cross the river by a bridge, and continue for another 1.5km to the point where the path begins to climb, a fence descends on the opposite bank and two rivers merge. Cross down to the river by a shieling, ford the Allt a'Coire Uaine and follow the Allt a'Choire Chaoil upstream.

The walking is not difficult, but there is not much of a path. Follow the burn for about 3km to the point where the glen steepens and the water cascades over a large boulder. Above this, continue to climb south to reach the spur and find the usual path to The Saddle from Glen Shiel. The Forcan Ridge soon begins, a fantastic scramble with towers and steep drops. The traverse can be as hard or easy as you like, but although most of the tricky sections are avoidable there is considerable exposure. From the top tower of the Forcan Ridge, there is a short difficult section in descent. (It is possible to explore variations on the north flank but these are also exposed and it is best to keep to the crest.) Climb more easily to the double summit of The Saddle

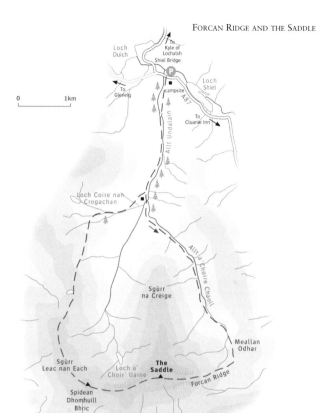

(GR935131) (5h). Descend to the west, following fenceposts to the smaller top of Spidean Dhomhuill Bhric. Continue north along the ridge with interest, over another top and then NNE down undulating terrain to eventually reach a small lochan nestling on the ridge. Contour northeast around the

next knoll for about 300m to a flatter area: if you look closely, you will find the remains of an old path. This leads NNE down grassy slopes to join a newer path by some trees and the burn from Loch Coire nan Crogachan. Follow this path to the glen, and return to Shiel Bridge (7h40).

◀ Beinn Sgritheall and The Saddle from Sgùrr Thionail

Sgritheall circuit

Beinn a'Chapuill (759m),
Beinn Sgritheall Ⓜ (928m)

Walk time **9h** Height gain **1200m**
Distance **23km** OS Map Landranger 33

**An unusual and intricate approach on
good paths and tracks to reach
entertaining ridges and two linked
peaks. Stamina is required to negotiate
rough terrain, particularly on descent.**

Start at the end of the public road in Glen
More, 8km east of Glenelg (GR880190).
(Park just east of the cattle grid at the start
of the plantation.) Take the private road
southeast to Moyle House and continue
southwards on a track beyond. Watch for a
gate on the right, 2km from the start.
Beyond the gate, take a track through the
trees and over a bridge. After the bridge,
leave the track and head west across bog
towards a solid wall and the Suardalan

Bothy beyond. This gives access to a good
path that leads southwards past a lochan,
where it becomes a track, and reaches a
junction at a gate. Continue straight on
(sign for Glen Beag) for about 600m. Look
out for a bridge hidden in the trees (at a
passing place on the right where the track
bends). Cross the river and climb through
trees to reach a stile. Follow the edge of
forestry, passing beneath the pylons, and
then start to climb grassy slopes WSW
along a good ridge. This soon levels out, but
then continues without mercy to the
warped plateau of Beinn a'Chapuill.
Continue to the far southwestern edge of
the plateau (the cliffs are steep on the
southeast flank), and descend grassy slopes
to reach Loch Bealach na h-Oidhche. Walk
east from the lochan to gain the easy-
angled north ridge of Beinn Sgritheall.
Higher up, the curving ridge gives exposed

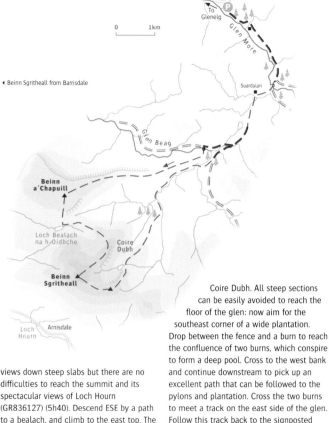

◀ Beinn Sgritheall from Barrisdale

views down steep slabs but there are no difficulties to reach the summit and its spectacular views of Loch Hourn (GR836127) (5h40). Descend ESE by a path to a bealach, and climb to the east top. The northeast ridge begins easily; lower down, a short section of awkward scree (keep to the east side to avoid crags) leads to a flat area near a lochan. Rise north over a knoll and descend the ridge as it continues east of

Coire Dubh. All steep sections can be easily avoided to reach the floor of the glen: now aim for the southeast corner of a wide plantation. Drop between the fence and a burn to reach the confluence of two burns, which conspire to form a deep pool. Cross to the west bank and continue downstream to pick up an excellent path that can be followed to the pylons and plantation. Cross the two burns to meet a track on the east side of the glen. Follow this track back to the signposted intersection. [Variant: if the rivers are in spate, cross by the footbridge used on your approach, just west of the plantation.] Return by the tracks and paths to Glen More (9h).

65

Old path to Glen Arnisdale

Druim Fada (713m)

Walk time **5h40** Height gain **900m**

Distance **14km** OS Map **Landranger 33**

A walk over varied terrain to gain a high ridge with views of Loch Hourn and Ladhar Bheinn. This route involves some steep sections, and good navigation is required for the descent.

Start at the end of the public road at the entrance to Corran by Loch Hourn (GR848095). Walk into the village and cross the bridge over the River Arnisdale. Just after the bridge, take the track on the left signposted for Kinlochhourn. Pass through two gates by the banks of the river and then strike out across grassy fields, following a faded track that passes some ruins. This becomes a path at a fence that can be crossed by a gate. Follow the river through birch and then join a track at a bridge. Keep to the south bank and follow the track for 2.5km as it wanders and then climbs through the glen. At the point where Dubh Lochain comes into view and the track drops to cross the river, leave the track: a burn cascades northwards through a tight ravine. Follow this burn on its east bank for about 150m towards the gulch. Before it closes up, trend leftwards

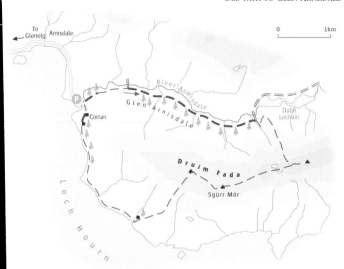

(northeast) over steep grassy slopes to gain the apex of a steep-sided ridge. Climb along this spur as it gains height steadily before steepening and then flattening in waves to the top of Druim Fada: this presents no difficulties. The summit cairn is a short way east, set above the highest of many knolls (GR894084) (3h). The next 2.5km west is a tough journey over and around a contorted maze of mounds and buttresses with some short rocky sections in descent and ascent, but the fine views of Loch Hourn and Ladhar Bheinn are ample reward. A grassy spur between two lochans makes a fine spot for lunch. After this, there are a couple of steep rises to gain Sgùrr Mór, the only named top. From

this point, most of the bumps can be turned to reach the final top, marked with a trig point snapped at the hilt. Descend SSW from here to take a vague ridge, keeping a set of crags to the north after 300m. Further down, where the hillside is scored with ravines, turn more to the west to reach the shore of Loch Hourn by a ruin. Follow an excellent path northwest along the coast, passing several bays piled with bright pebbles. On approaching Corran, watch for a gate in the first fence you reach. Pass through the gate and around the front of a green shed, and follow the farm track through two more gates into Corran and back to the start (5h40).

◄ Loch Hourn and Druim Fada from Sgùrr a'Mhaoraich

67

The Sisterhood

Sgùrr a'Bhealaich Dheirg ⓜ (1036m),
Saileag ⓜ (956m),
Sgùrr na Ciste Duibhe ⓜ (1027m),
Sgùrr na Carnach ⓜ (1002m),
Sgùrr Fhuaran ⓜ (1067m),
Sgùrr nan Saighead (929m)

Walk time **10h20** Height gain **1800m**
Distance **30km** OS Map **Landranger 33**

A spectacular rocky ridge with some exposure and tricky though short-lived sections in ascent and descent.

Start from the Kintail National Trust for Scotland Centre at Morvich (GR960210). (Some parking here; also at Ault a'chruinn.)

Walk east along the road for 600m until signs point to a track bearing southeast to Alltbeithe. Follow the track for about 6km until you reach the Hadden Woodburn Memorial Hut (private). Take an excellent path from the hut to cross the Allt an Lapain and the ravine of the Allt Grannda by two bridges. The path leads east, gaining height easily into a chasm with three waterfalls before levelling off and undulating towards the watershed at Cnoc Biodaig. At the highest point, leave the path and start to climb southwards along the spur of Streath a'Ghlas-choire, which becomes more pronounced higher up. This

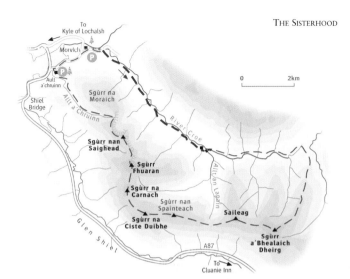

terrain is rockier and more exposed towards the top, but most tricky sections can be easily bypassed. The ridge culminates in an amazing cairn on the summit of Sgùrr a'Bhealaich Dheirg (GR035144) (5h40). Follow the ridge westwards, dropping slightly to reach Saileag and further again to Bealach an Lapain. [Escape: descend north from the bealach to the corrie, and follow the west bank of the Allt an Lapain to the hut.] From this point, climb steeply west over numerous false summits with wild drops to the north. At the top of Sgùrr nan Spainteach, there is a tricky step to descend: this gives access to a curious hidden bowl before the rocky summit of Sgùrr na Ciste Duibhe (GR984159) (7h40). Descend by the northwest ridge to a bealach, then climb Sgùrr na Carnach.

Leave this peak by its north ridge and begin the long and steep south face of Sgùrr Fhuaran to the summit (GR978167). The descent is a little tricky: drop NNW for 200m before a path leads northwards to join a sharp ridge down to a bealach. Climb NNW along a ridge that overlooks vast slabs to reach the summit of Sgùrr nan Saighead. Drop to the northwest and then climb over the rocky buttress of Beinn Bhuidhe before descending to a bealach shared with Sgùrr na Moraich. Leave the ridge by descending on the west, and follow a path on the right bank of the Allt a'Chruinn over boggy ground. Later, the path improves and loops northeast to avoid steep ground near a waterfall before leading to a minor road above Ault a'chruinn. It is a short walk back to the start (10h20).

◀ The Five Sisters from the road to Glenelg

Beinn Fhada massif

A'Ghlas-bheinn ⓜ (918m),
Beinn Fhada ⓜ (1032m)

Walk time **10h** Height gain **1600m**
Distance **23km** OS Map **Landranger 33**

**A long climb over the peaks of this
great massif. Scrambling skills and
plenty of stamina will add to enjoyment
on this route.**

Start at the Kintail National Trust for
Scotland Centre at Morvich (GR960210).
(Limited parking.) Walk east along the
private road to reach the bridge after 1km.
Cross this, and follow signs on the left for
the Falls of Glomach. Walk west of the
houses at Innis a'Chròtha and northeast
along Strath Croe by a good path. Pass
through a gate after 1km, and reach an
intersection and sign about 300m beyond.
Follow a minor path down to the river
where a bridge leads you to a grassy track.
Take the track northwards past Dorusduain
and along the glen, much of it now
harvested for trees. The track crosses a
rickety bridge and becomes a path, turning
to climb east and keeping high above the
Allt an Leòid Ghaineamhaich before
levelling out at Bealach na Sròine. Just
beyond an old wall, two cairns mark a
divergence of paths. Take the right variant:
an old route makes a rising traverse
clockwise around Meall Dubh. Follow this
for 400m until it peters out and then climb
southwest up the ridge to the undulating
top of Meall Dubh. Walk south, pass a
lochan and climb Creag na Saobhie. Drop

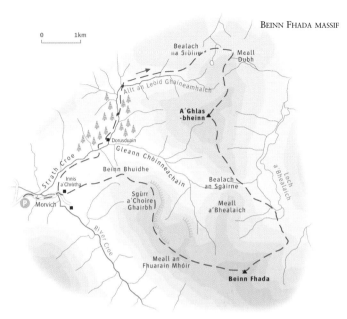

slightly to tackle the final steep slopes to the summit of A'Ghlas-bheinn (GR008231) (4h20). A well-defined path descends SSE over numerous small knolls to reach Bealach an Sgàirne. [Escape: descend west along Gleann Chòinneachain.] Drop southeastwards along an excellent path towards Gleann Gniomhaidh. At the south end of Loch a'Bhealaich, leave the path and bear diagonally southeast up grassy slopes (a grassy rake is good to follow) to reach the prominent northeast ridge of Beinn Fhada. Follow this spur with interest to the summit (GR018193). (6h40). Descend gently WNW over a vast plateau. Climb to Meall an Fhuarain-Mhóir, the west summit, where the fun begins. The northwest ridge offers

spectacular views, some exposure and a short section of scrambling. Descend WNW direct from the summit: the ridge dips and crests many times with steep drops, especially on the north aspect. The peak of Sgùrr a'Choire Ghairbh starts with a 20m scramble and continues over seemingly impossible terrain: a series of rocky spurs that each require ascent and descent (keep to the high ground). The ridge then drops in stages to reach the grassy Beinn Bhuidhe. Descend west along the spur to meet a deer fence. Take the gate just to the left of the spur and cross the heathery terrain below, aiming just left of the white houses of Innis a'Chròtha. Two gates lead you out to the road and back to the start (10h).

◀ Cliffs of Sgùrr a'Choire Ghairbh on Beinn Fhada

71

The Benula Triangle

Mullach na Dheiragain Ⓜ (982m),
Sgùrr nan Ceathreamhan Ⓜ (1151m),
An Socach Ⓜ (921m)

Walk time **8h** Height gain **1400m**
Approach and return **3h bike or 5h20 walk**
Distance **19km + 20km approach and
return** OS Map **Landranger 25**

**Exciting ridge walk with some exposure,
rough ground and interesting route-
finding. This circuit is best accessed by
mountain bike.**

Start from the entrance to the Killilan
Estate at a sharp bend in the road
(GR940304). (Large parking area here.) Walk
or cycle east along the private road,
through Killilan and along Glen Elchaig. The
tarmac gives way to gravel after 3km but
the surface is still excellent. Continue to
the head of Loch na Leitreach at Carnach,
reached after 10km. Leave bikes here: walk
times start from this point. Take the track
behind the house, which leads south to a
bridge across the Allt na Doire Gairbhe.
Follow the track along the Allt Coire

Easaich, which can form a fine waterfall in
spate, and climb steeply eastwards up a
vague rib. After the track switches back, the
terrain levels out. Leave the track here
rather than follow it to Creag Ghlas, and
head ENE directly across the moor aiming
for a knoll just below the steep upper
section of Sgùrr na h-Eige. Just past the
knoll, an almost continuous grassy ramp
leads down to flatter, marshy ground close
to Loch an Droma. Keep to the south of a
large moraine and gain a grassy track about
600m beyond. [Variant from Carnach: walk
up the glen to Iron Lodge, cross the river
and climb east by the track towards Loch
Mullardoch. Pass over the bealach and
watch for a grassy track that crosses the
river by a new bridge.] Follow the track to
cross the Abhainn Sithidh by a bridge.
Climb Creag a'Choir'Aird directly: the rough
slopes give way to broken crags towards the
top, marked with a cairn. Continue more
easily along the wide ridge to Mullach
Sithidh, and then skirt around the steep
corrie to reach the summit of Mullach na
Dheiragain (GR080259) (3h40). Continue
easily along the main ridge and climb Carn

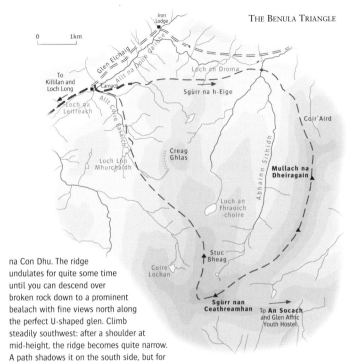

na Con Dhu. The ridge undulates for quite some time until you can descend over broken rock down to a prominent bealach with fine views north along the perfect U-shaped glen. Climb steadily southwest: after a shoulder at mid-height, the ridge becomes quite narrow. A path shadows it on the south side, but for some mild exposure you can climb the gnarled apex directly to reach the summit of Sgùrr nan Ceathreamhan (GR057228) (5h40). [Variant: descend the east ridge to An Socach and then continue to Glen Affric Youth Hostel to make a two-day adventure.] Descend the rocky west ridge with care to a windy bealach, and climb to the west top. Walk northwest for about 150m to reach a line of fenceposts. Follow these northwards, down to a minor bealach and over Stuc Bheag. Descend and climb a second knoll beyond. Begin to make a slow northwest

descent from here towards Loch Lòn Mhurchaidh, following an easy grassy line to keep south of the steep slabs of Creag Ghlas. Cross the boggy flats to the foot of the lochan where a path takes you northeast to another older path (hard to find) that descends north close to the exit burn. This path drops steeply with many tight hairpins above the cascades of the Allt Coire Easaich: in a few places it has crumbled away and care is required. This leads down to your original track to Carnach (8h). Walk or pedal back to the start.

◂ Loch a'Bhealaich and the southern slopes of Sgùrr nan Ceathreamhan

73

Ben Killilan above Loch Long

Sguman Coinntich ⑩(879m),
Ben Killilan (753m)

Walk time 5h20 + detour 40 min
Height gain 800m Distance 16km
OS Map Landranger 25

A mountain horseshoe over Loch Long. The higher peak involves some steep ascent and descent as an avoidable detour. Good navigation is required.

Start from the entrance to the Killilan Estate, at a sharp bend in the road (GR940304). (Large parking area here.) Walk east along the private road to Killilan. About 30m beyond the phone box, two tracks on the left of the road serve the back and front of a house. Take the track on the right, which leads to the front and a path through the trees. Follow this path as it rises between the Allt a'Choire Mhóir and a wall to meet a gate. Beyond the gate, turn left and pass through a second rusty gate by a stand of old pine. Continue by a path to reach a junction of tracks after about 500m. Go straight on to follow an excellent grassy track as it gains height into Coire Mór, giving great views back across Loch Long. When the track ends higher up, continue eastwards over rough slopes to reach Bealach Mhic Bheathain set below steep cliffs (2h20). [Detour: climb steeply southwest from just below the bealach on the Coire Mór side, noting the easiest line through broken buttresses and along scree runnels. The ridge then leads more easily to the summit of Sguman Coinntich

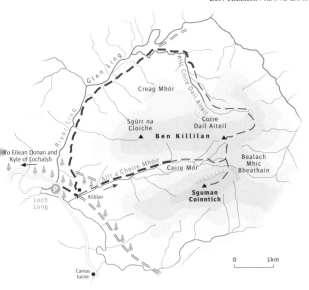

(GR977303). Return to the bealach, taking care not to descend towards vertical terrain further east (add 40 min.).] Walk north over a knoll and steeply down, then across uneven ground NNE to another hummock. This marks the east extreme of Ben Killilan, a wide and undulating ridge with several high points, any of which should count as the summit. From this top, descend ENE along a good ridge. This leads to a lochan with a huddle of boulders at its edge. Follow the outlet burn through Coire Dail Aiteil to join a grassy track. This soon turns to gravel, making a steep zigzag descent towards the crazy loop of the River Ling. After passing the waterfalls of the Allt Coire Dail Aiteil, bear west across the boggier reaches to gain another gravel track along Glen Ling. Follow this into Killilan, and return to the start (5h20).

Otters

Scotland is one of few countries with a thriving otter population. The local species is the Eurasian Otter, whose habitat extended from the UK to Japan and from Finland to North Africa, although in many areas it is now extinct. It was only in 1982 that they became a protected species in Scotland. There is an otter sanctuary in Kylerhea, across Loch Alsh, where visitors can view some of the local families at close quarters, if they are lucky.

◂ The narrows of Loch Long from Allt nan-sugh

Attadale adventure

Bidean a'Choire Sheasgaich ⓜ (945m),
Lurg Mhór ⓜ (986m)

Walk time 6h40 + detour 40 min
Height gain 1000m
Approach and return 3h bike or 5h40 walk
Distance 15km + 22km approach and
return OS Map Landranger 25

**Long approach to reach two high peaks
with a ravine and waterfalls. Scrambling
skills would help on steep and exposed
ground. This route is best accessed by
mountain bike, and can be spread over
two days for an easier trip.**

Start 500m south of the railway station in
Attadale on Loch Carron at the entrance to
Attadale Gardens, where there is parking for
walkers (GR924387). Walk or cycle along

the private road, which bends northeast to a
house and forks just beyond. Turn right
towards the holiday cottages and continue
southeast along the glen. The track soon
turns to gravel, crosses the river and starts
to climb. Where the track forks, after a first
descent, take the left turn to continue
uphill. After considerable effort this takes
you to a bealach, and it is downhill almost
all of the way to the refurbished Bendronaig
Lodge and bothy. Leave bikes here: walk
times start from this point. Follow a track
east from the bothy down to a burn and
cross this by the wire bridge. Now take the
track that leads north above the Black
Water to Loch an Laoigh. This ends on
reaching a broad burn flowing from the east.
Climb rough terrain to follow the tumbling

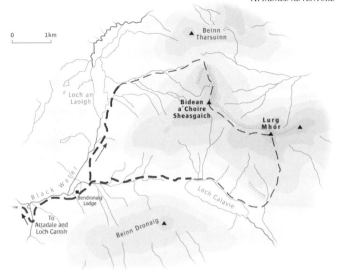

0   1km

Loch an Laoigh

Beinn Tharsuinn ▲

Bidean a'Choire Sheasgaich ▲

Lurg Mhór ▲

Black Water

Bendronaig Lodge

To Attadale and Loch Carron

Loch Calavie

Beinn Dronaig ▲

water – even more impressive higher up – into a fine ravine about 30m deep and almost narrow enough to jump across. At the top of the ravine, cross the burn easily and continue to a wide bealach and old wall south of Beinn Tharsuinn. Follow the wall southwards towards the imposing north ridge of Bidean a'Choire Sheasgaich. Where the wall ends, continue to climb SSE for about 60m in height over broken rocky ground to reach a grassy terrace, following a vague path. Do not be tricked into trending right as this ends in hard moves on poor quality rock; instead, follow the terrace left. This gains an easy gully to reach a boulderfield below the main band of cliffs. Ascend a gully and exposed path to the right of these crags to reach the easier

terrain above. Bear south over undulating ground and crisscrossed rocks to tackle the final slopes to the summit of Bidean a'Choire Sheasgaich (GR049413) (3h40). Continue south for about 100m, and then begin an easy southeasterly descent to a prominent bealach. Climb east in several waves to reach the summit of Lurg Mhór (GR065404) (4h40). [Detour: the journey to the east top is an entertaining scramble. Return to the main summit (add 40 min).] Descend SSE from the summit, along a vague ridgeline. Lower down, trend south to follow the watercourse towards the foot of Loch Calavie. A path leads along the shore and then westwards over a bealach as a track, descending to the wire bridge near Bendronaig Lodge (6h40). Use your remaining energy to return to the start.

◄ Attadale from Loch Carron

To the west of Loch Ness, these parallel glens are home to what is arguably the greatest concentration of high peaks in Scotland as well as one of the largest ancient Caledonian pinewoods. Sinuous single-track roads lead deep into a land of loch, moorland and mountain: home for many rare birds, animals and plants. If lucky, you may see golden eagles, merlins and pine martens on your travels.

Three of the routes start in Glen Affric: a shorter walk takes the lower hills to the south of Loch Affric, and a mammoth trek tackles the giants on the north side. Another route with some scrambling begins at the Glen Affric Youth Hostel, buried deep in the mountains. One long walk starts at Loch Mullardoch and another circuit takes in Glen Strathferrar, best approached by bike. A shorter route to a hidden lochan starts at the head of Strathconon. Two walks of very different character take off from Achnashellach to climb the hills of Monar: one rounded, the other rugged.

Glen Affric to Loch Monar

The Sassenach's spur

Aonach Shasuinn (888m)

Walk time **6h40** Height gain **700m**
Distance **20km**
OS Maps **Landranger 25 and 34**

A route that begins with good tracks and paths from Glen Affric to reach a fine ridge and less visited hills. Rough ground higher up means stamina and good navigation are important.

Start at the end of the public road and car park in Glen Affric (GR201233). From the west end of the car park, follow a path that descends to a track and bridge. Cross the bridge and follow the track westwards and through a gate to reach an intersection. Take the right fork and walk through the old forest of Pollan Buidhe. After 1km, pass through another gate, at which point you can see Affric Lodge, and walk for a further 500m to a signpost for Cougie. Leave the track here to follow a path southwards through the sparse Caledonian pine that lines the east bank of the Allt Garbh. Occasionally the path fades but the terrain is not difficult. Beyond some fenceposts after 1km, continue close to the burn for a further 500m. As the glen widens, leave the

burn to join a track that seems to appear from nowhere. Follow the track more easily upstream to reach a wooden bridge. Cross to the other side and make your way along the grassy track that leads to a locked shed overlooking Loch an Sgùid. Continue up the glen over difficult and boggy terrain for 1km, until you have passed the wild meandering of the Allt Garbh. Ford the burn without difficulty here and ascend heathery slopes to Bealach an Amais. Turn east from the bealach, and climb the west ridge to the double summit of Aonach Shasuinn to enjoy fine views of the Glen Affric peaks (GR173180) (4h). Descend easily ESE to a bealach, and walk northeast along the undulating ridge of Carn nan Coireachan Cruaidh. Drop down to the north, aiming for Cnap na Stri. Climb this knoll and continue a northwards

descent for about 500m, before bearing northwest over rough ground to reach the track above the Allt Garbh. Follow this track rather than the burn, but when the track turns east towards Cougie leave it and bear northwest to rejoin your original approach above the water. Retrace your steps into Glen Affric and back to the start (6h40).

Sassenachs

The word *Sasunn* means 'England' in Gaelic, and those from England are known in Scots as *Sassenachs*. It is thought, therefore, that Aonach Shasuinn may have been named after some southern visitors, possibly Hanoverian soldiers.

◀ Aonach Shasuinn from Carn nan Coireachan Cruaidh

Wild night out in Affric

Mullach Fraoch choire ⓜ(1102m),
A'Chralaig ⓜ(1120m)

Walk time **9h** Height gain **1200m**
Distance **24km**
OS Maps Landranger **25, 33 and 34**

**A high ridge linking two fine peaks with
scrambling and exposure along the way.
Plenty of stamina is required for a steep
initial section and a long return by paths
and tracks in remote country.**

Start at the Glen Affric Youth Hostel
(GR079202). Walk south from the hostel and
cross the bridge over the River Affric. Follow
the river downstream for about 800m to the
edge of a deer fence, and then bear south to
climb a steep grassy spur to the west side of

the Allt Dubh. This gains height quickly,
leading to a cairn at the top of a knoll.
Climb gentle grassy slopes southeast to join
the north ridge of Mullach Fraoch choire.
Follow the spur southwards to reach the
summit with ease. Descend by the south
ridge: a path leads on the west side to
avoid an initial steep section, but then the
ridge becomes very narrow and cannot be
avoided. A short section of easy scrambling
is best taken directly along the crest.
Reaching the top of the first rocky castle
provides the crux, after which the route is
exposed for a short time but not difficult.
The narrow ridge is then taken on the west
side to lead easily down to a bealach. Climb
Stob Coire na Cralaig and then continue

◀ The southeast ridge of A'Chralaig

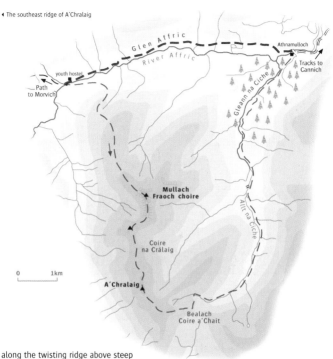

along the twisting ridge above steep corries, climbing steadily to the summit of A'Chralaig (GR094148) (4h20). Descend steeply southeast and continue over much flatter ground. Where the ridge steepens again, bear east to take a prominent spur. This becomes rocky lower down and reaches the wide Bealach Coire a'Chait. At the first dip you encounter on the bealach, look for some slabs on the northwest side. From these, an old path leads northwards, heading to the left out of sight around a

rocky nose before dropping in zigzags down to the glen. This path continues on the west bank of the Allt na Ciche, before crossing to the east after about 1km. Follow it down as it becomes first a grassy track and then, after rounding the bulk of A'Chioch, a gravel track. This can be followed down through the glen to Athnamulloch in Glen Affric. Head east for Cannich or west back to the hostel (9h).

Peaks of Glen Affric

Màm Sodhail ⓜ (1181m), **Carn Eige** ⓜ (1183m), **Beinn Fhionnlaidh** ⓜ (1005m), **Tom a'Chòinich** ⓜ (1112m), **Toll Creagach** ⓜ (1053m)

Walk time **8h20** + detour 2h
Height gain **1400m** Distance **24km**
OS Map Landranger 25

A challenging ridge walk over many high peaks accessed on good paths but requiring stamina and good navigation. Extra peaks can be added en route for those with plenty of energy.

Start at the end of the public road and car park in Glen Affric (GR201233). Two tracks lead west from here: take the upper track towards Affric Lodge. Pass the entrance to the lodge, and continue west along the excellent path above the north bank of Loch Affric. Watch for a path on the right about 3km beyond the lodge and just before the Allt Coire Leachavie. Then climb steeply and without respite, bearing northwest through Coire Leachavie to emerge at a bealach between Ciste Dhubh and Màm Sodhail. Bear northeast to climb easily to the summit cairn of Màm Sodhail (GR120253) (4h20). Descend the north ridge to a bealach and continue around the corrie to the summit of Carn Eige. [Detour: drop northwest down a defined grassy ridge to reach Bealach Beag, before rising over gentle slopes to the summit of Beinn Fhionnlaidh. Return to the summit of Carn Eige (add 2h).] Descend the wide east ridge, rise over a knoll and continue around Coire Domhain before dropping steeply over scree to Garbh-bealach. Climb northeast to two

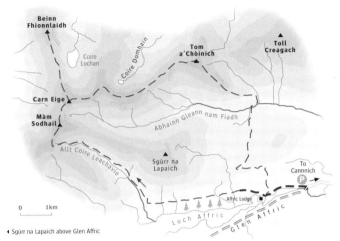

◄ Sgùrr na Lapaich above Glen Affric

smaller tops with a set of sheer cliffs on the southern flank, before the last short climb along fenceposts to the summit of Tom a'Chòinich. Descend the excellent southeast ridge by a slender path. Lower down, this winds through the rocks and slabs at Creag na h-Inghinn before reaching a main path which serves the Bealach Toll Easa. Drop to meet the Abhainn Gleann nam Fiadh and walk upstream to cross the water after about 300m. (If the river is in spate, follow it downstream to emerge on the road further east.) Find a grassy track that leads

south over the moor. This soon trends west and then doubles back before dropping into Glen Affric, emerging near Affric Lodge a short distance from the start (8h20). [Variant: from the summit of Tom a'Chòinich, descend the east ridge to Bealach Toll Easa and then climb over two humps to the summit of Toll Creagach. Descend southwards from the top, walk over Beinn Eun and drop steeply down to the track. Head south through the Coille Meallan reserve and down to the road. It is 1.5km back to the start (add 1h).]

Caledonian forest

Some 10,000 years ago, forest – mainly Caledonian pine – covered almost half of Scotland. Over the centuries trees were cleared for fuel and building materials, and to remove cover that sheltered wolves. More recently, the iron foundries, sheep farming and demand for materials during the wars have left very few extensive stands of original forest. The current work of Forest Enterprise, including the planting of native mixed forest, aims to regenerate the natural woodland environment.

A Glencannich trek

Carn nan Gobhar (992m),
Sgùrr na Lapaich (1150m),
An Riabhachan (1129m),
An Socach (1069m)

Walk time **8h20** Height gain **1100m**
Distance **21km** OS Map Landranger 25

A long excursion into high and rugged mountains with plenty of ascent. The route can be extended to take in more hills for those seeking an additional challenge.

Start from the end of the public road at the foot of Loch Mullardoch by Benula Lodge (GR219316). Walk west past the boathouse and take any one of the boggy paths and tracks that lead westwards to meet the Allt Mullardoch by a bridge after 1km. Turn north and climb up through the glen, following a path close to the river. After 2km on this path, and just before a burn, start to climb eastwards. Heather soon turns to rocky terrain, which takes you to a more prominent ridge above Coire na Buidheig. Descend northwards over various knolls to meet a bealach with a wall. Climb northwest to the summit of Creag Dubh (GR199351) (3h). Descend gently along the

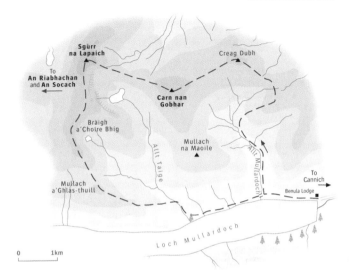

broad ridge to a bealach, before climbing to the top of Carn nan Gobhar on the north side of the summit plateau. Descend WNW to Bealach na Chloiche Duibhe: these scree-laden slopes start awkwardly but further down become grassy and strewn with large boulders. This aspect of Sgùrr na Lapaich is quite dramatic, with deep corries and pronounced ridges. Begin the arduous climb up the east ridge. For added excitement near the top, you can keep to the rocky apex above Coire nan Each rather than easier terrain to the left: both take you to the summit (GR161351) (5h20). Descend southwards to take the great ridge of Bràigh a'Choire Bhig down to the knoll of Mullach a'Ghlas-thuill. Follow the east ridge until this becomes too complex to do so with

ease. Drop north into the corrie and maintain an easterly direction to meet the Allt Taige with rapids over rusted slabs. Cross the burn and pick up a path down to Loch Mullardoch. [Variant: descend southwest from Sgùrr na Lapaich to Bealach Toll an Lochain and begin another long climb to An Riabhachan with one narrow section over steep cliffs. Follow the long summit ridge, which is shaped like a giant ice axe, for almost 2km until it divides abruptly to the left and right. Descend to Bealach Bholla and climb the reclusive An Socach. Descend by the southeast ridge over Meall a'Chasig, and drop to the Allt Coire a'Mhaim. Accompany the burn down to Loch Mullardoch (add 4h)]. Follow the shores back to the start (8h20).

◀ Sgùrr na Lapaich from Creag Dubh

Strathferrar Horseshoe

Sgùrr na Ruaidhe (993m), **Carn nan Gobhar** (992m), **Sgùrr a'Choire Ghlais** (1083m), **Sgùrr Fhuar-thuill** (1049m)

Walk time **8h** Height gain **1500m**
Approach and return **2h20 bike**
Distance **24km + 26km approach and return** OS Maps **Landranger 25 and 26**

A demanding route over many tops on mostly good paths, accessed by bike to journey deep into the hills. Care is needed on the final descent.

Start at the Scottish Natural Heritage car park just west of the village of Struy (GR395406). Cycle west along the private tarmac road for 11km, passing Loch Beannacharain. Look for a track on the right

1km after the Deanie Power Station (GR284386). Leave bikes here: walk times start from this point. Take the track northwards as it zigzags steeply to a weir. Now continue along a mix of grassy tracks and paths that follow the east bank of the Allt Coire Mhuillidh. After 3km, a minor burn comes down from the east. Cross this and start to bear northeast over even grass slopes. These lead eventually to a rough shelter and the summit of Sgùrr na Ruaidhe (GR289426) (2h40). Descend easily northwest to a bealach, climb north over undulating rocky ground and then arc west over the plateau to the summit of Carn nan Gobhar. This is set back to the north of the peak and gives spectacular views. Descend southwest to a prominent bealach, and then begin the steep haul up the defined ridge to the summit of Sgùrr a'Choire Ghlais (GR258430) (4h40). Descend northwest to another bealach before threading your way through rocks and following the rim of the corrie to the top of Creag Ghorm a'Bhealaich. This leaves only one major peak on the ridge: Sgùrr Fhuar-thuill is easily reached and it is only a short traverse to its satellite, Sgùrr na Fearstaig. From this point, descend the south ridge overlooking Loch Toll a'Mhuic before the final push to

the top of Sgùrr na Muice (GR226417) (6h20). Walk 50m west from the summit cairn to avoid cliffs and then descend due south. The terrain is quite awkward with folds, scree and slabs but soon leads to a flat area before the knolls of Carn an Daimh Bhàin. Descend east by a burn, and then tramp southeast over heather to meet a good path by the Allt Toll a'Mhuic. Further south, this becomes a track and joins the tarmac road in the glen. Walk east towards the Deanie Power Station (8h). Freewheel back to the start.

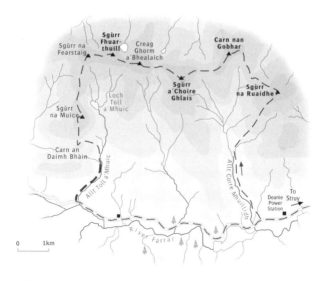

◄ Sgùrr a'Choire Ghlais and the peaks of Strathferrar

Strathconon lochans

Bac an Eich ⓒ (849m)

Walk time **6h20** Height gain **900m**
Distance **17km** OS Map **Landranger 25**

**Good tracks lead to wilder country to
climb a single peak by two steep ridges.
Rough ground in ascent is rewarded by
an easy return through a hidden glen.**

Start near the head of Loch
Beannacharain at the end of the public road
along Strathconon (GR225519). Walk west
along the private road, past Scardroy Lodge
and the monument to General John
Frederick Boyce Combe to reach Corrievuic

after 2.5km. Cross the River Meig by the
bridge to reach two old ruins. Start to climb
ESE along the prominent crest of Creag
Achadh an Eas. An old track assists your
ascent for part of this section above an
impressive ravine. The track then turns
south into a mire of bog: it is better to keep
to the rough apex of the ridge and gain the
top of Meall Buidhe. Walk south to a
second bump and begin an easy descent to
reach the head of Loch Toll Lochain. Turn
the lochan on its southern side to avoid the
maze of peaty groughs at its foot, passing
beneath the cold eastern corrie. Begin an

ascent of Sgùrr Toll Lochain, climbing steep heathery runnels to gain the much flatter ridge higher up. Follow the ridge to the summit of Bac an Eich (GR222489) (4h20). Descend WSW over easy slopes: these become steeper to follow the vague ridge of Drochaid Coire Mhadaidh down to a bealach. A good grassy track descends northwest into Coire Mhóraigein; lower down the track becomes a narrow path, wheels around the north side of Creag Coire na Feola and returns to the ruins. Take the track back to the start (6h20).

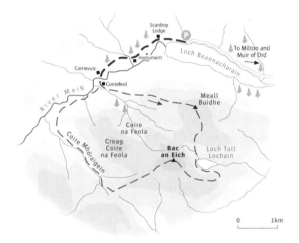

Lochs, lochans and bog

The Highlands have the largest individual bodies of water in Britain by area (Loch Lomond), by volume (Loch Ness) and by depth (Loch Morar, at 310m deep the 17th deepest in the world). There are about 4500 lochs in Scotland and it is estimated that there are more than 150,000 smaller lochans, ponds and pools. There are also extensive areas of both blanket bog and raised bog, which hold huge amounts of water within the peat. Of all the freshwater in the British Isles, therefore, Scotland is estimated to possess around 70% by area and 90% by volume.

◄ Loch Toll Lochain below Bac an Eich

Two from Achnashellach

Sgùrr nan Ceannaichean ⓜ(915m),
Moruisg ⓜ(928m)

Walk time **4h20** Height gain **1100m**
Approach and return **1h20 bike or 3h walk**
Distance **11km + 12km approach and
return** OS Map **Landranger 25**

**Two rewarding peaks and a fine ridge
gained from a reclusive glen. A bike will
save time and make for an exhilarating
return. This walk can be linked with
even higher peaks described in the next
route: Mountains of Monar.**
    Start from Achnashellach Forest car park,
400m east of Gerry's Hostel (GR040494).

Cross the railway by the gate just opposite
the car park, and walk or cycle east along
the gravel track beside the railway for
800m. Cross the River Carron to reach a
junction. Bear east (left) and start to gain
height, ignoring a small turning after 1km
that descends to the river. The route drops
after a while and follows the Allt a'Chonais
closely. Watch for an old path leading north,
300m east of the point where the Allt
Leathad an Tobair and Allt a'Chonais meet.
Mountain bikes are best left here: walk
times start from this point. The path is not
always easy to find or follow and these
slopes give a steep ascent of the peak.
Higher up, the terrain eases and

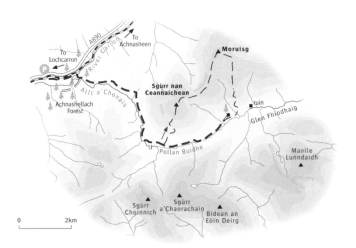

some gentle climbing in a northeasterly direction takes you to the summit of Sgùrr nan Ceannaichean (GR087481) (1h40). The hidden northern corries of the massif are quite steep and the ridge gives a fine walk. Descend northeast and then east to a bealach above Coire an Tuill Bhàin, then continue around the cirque to the wide summit plateau of Moruisg.

Descend easily southeast over grasses, aiming for a smaller knoll on the ridge. Then, before rising any further, drop due south. This soon reaches a good path that twists its way steeply into the glen, reaching the flats just east of Glenuaig Lodge. Walk west to the lodge and pick up the track that leads west along the glen (4h20). Cycle or walk back to the start.

Sea lochs

Sea lochs, like Loch Carron, are flooded glens formed when vast ice sheets melted and caused a global rise in sea levels. These saltwater lochs are unique to Scotland and can stretch for many miles inland. They create a very diverse ecosystem with marine life that is not found elsewhere. The narrow inlets closer to the sea can create tidal rapids where the water rushes in or out with great force.

◀ Looking west along Glen Fhiodhaig from Strathconon

Mountains of Monar

Maoile Lunndaidh (1007m),
Sgùrr a'Chaorachain (1053m),
Sgùrr Choinnich (999m)

Walk time **7h40** Height gain **1400m**
Approach and return **1h20 bike or 3h walk**
Distance **20km + 12km approach and
return** OS Map **Landranger 25**

**An excellent ridge route in remote
country, with a river crossing and some
exposure. Good navigation skills are
required and a mountain bike would
save some time on approach.**
  Start from Achnashellach Forest car park,
400m east of Gerry's Hostel (GR040494).

Cross the railway by the gate just opposite
the car park and walk or cycle east along
the gravel track beside the railway for
800m. Cross the River Carron to reach a
junction. Bear east (left) and start to gain
height, ignoring a small turning after 1km
that descends to the river. The route drops
after a while and follows the Allt a'Chonais
closely. At Pollan Buidhe, the river flows
from the east and is joined by a burn from
Bealach Bhearnais. Mountain bikes are best
left here: walk times start from this point.
Continue on foot along the glen for 3km to
Glenuaig Lodge, and pass it to reach an old
ruin after 1km. Cross to the south side of

the river and bear southeast to join the west ridge of Creag Dhubh Mhór. Follow this spur, steeply at first, alongside a waterfall. Soon the route eases and gives fine views of the complex crags and lochans of Fuar-tholl Mór. Traverse south to start the north ridge of Maoile Lunndaidh, and continue easily to the vast plateau at its summit (GR135458) (3h20). Walk southwest to a small knoll with cliffs on either side, and then bear WNW to Carn nam Fiaclan. Descend the west ridge to Drochaid Mhuilich, with views of Loch Monar and the imposing cliffs of Bidean an Eòin Deirg. Climb westwards across bog and by a burn

to Lochan Gaineamhach before joining Sròn na Frianich, the northeast ridge of Sgùrr a'Chaorachain, which leads to the summit (GR087447) (5h40). Follow the west ridge down to a bealach, which feels quite exposed, and ascend steeply WSW to the long summit of Sgùrr Choinnich. Lose height easily along the west ridge to a high bealach and then northwards to the lower Bealach Bhearnais. Find a path on the north bank of the Allt Leathad an Tobair which drops down to the glen. Cross the Allt a'Chonais by a wire bridge to reach the track (7h40). Walk or freewheel back to the start.

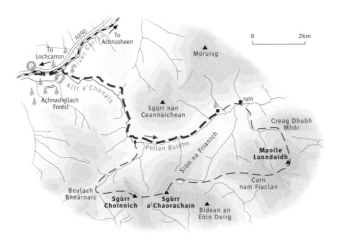

Index

ⓜ **Munros** are mountains in Scotland above 914m (3000ft). (Named after Sir Hugh Munro who compiled the first list in 1891.)

ⓒ **Corbetts** are peaks between 762m and 914m (2500ft and 3000ft) which have a drop of at least 152m (500ft) on all sides. (Named after John Corbett who drew up the list and made the first ascent.)